THE BOOKS OF RUTH AND ESTHER

A Study Manual

by

C. Reuben Anderson

BAKER BOOK HOUSE
Grand Rapids, Michigan

DEDICATED

to
my wife
Marjorie
and our four children
Karin, Wendell, Connie, Warren
who are the most wonderful family
a Pastor could ever have

FOREWORD

It has been a most rewarding and profitable experience for me to undertake the writing of this commentary on the Old Testament books of Ruth and Esther.

I have sought to develop a simple homiletical and exegetical outline study of the books. The use of alliteration has been employed in the outlines in an effort to aid in the mastery of the contents of the books. It is hoped that this aid does not seem too artificial or mechanical. I have also incorporated practical illustrative material, believing with Dwight L. Moody that "what windows are to a home, illustrations are to a sermon." They help to let the light in.

It is my prayer that God may be pleased to make the study of these beautiful books of the Bible both profitable and productive.

C. Reuben Anderson

Minneapolis, Minnesota
October, 1969

CONTENTS

THE BOOK OF RUTH

THE BOOK OF ESTHER

THE BOOK OF RUTH

Chapter 1

THE BOOK OF RUTH ANALYZED

I. THE NAME

The name Ruth means "pity or compassion," "sorrow or grief." The Book of Ruth in the Bible receives its name from "the young Moabitish widow who made Israel's people her people and Israel's God her God, and became an ancestress of the Messiah."[1]

Ruth did not belong to the Hebrew nationality, the nation of the Messiah, but was of the Moabite nation. It is of interest to note that the Moabites were descendants of Lot and therefore came from the same Semitic stock as did the patriarch Abraham. In the book of Genesis the Sethite line of descendants may be traced to Shem and Arphaxad which leads to Abraham. Through Lot of that genealogy have descended the Moabites.

The Book of Ruth has been described as "a biographical episode in a history."[2] The book presents an interlude in the midst of scenes of conflict and strife pictured in the book of Judges which it follows. It is a pleasant interlude of a pastoral life with faith, love, and devotion evidenced in the experiences of the chief characters who witness to the faithfulness of God.

II. THE NARRATIVE

Chapter 1 of the book begins the story with the words "And (now) it came to pass" (1:1). The scene is set during the days of the Judges, a very checkered period in Israel's history when as the record says, "every man did that which was right in his own eyes" (Judg. 21:25). To further complicate the situation "there was a famine in the land" (1:1). Apparently even the most fertile areas such as Bethlehem, which means "the house of bread," were in desperate need. Elimelech, who resided in Bethlehem, determined to take his family and move to the nearby nation of Moab where there was food to be secured. He

---

[1] Dickson, *The New Analytical Bible,* Chicago, 1941, p. 333.
[2] Pulpit Commentary, Vol. 8, Chicago, "Introduction to the Book of Ruth."

13

took with him his wife Naomi, and his two sons Mahlon and Chilion. The record seems to indicate that Elimelech met death very soon after taking up residence in Moab. Following his untimely departure, the two sons married Moabitish wives whose names were Orpah and Ruth.

After some ten years when apparently all was well with them, suddenly both Mahlon and Chilion passed away. One could readily believe that there was some constitutional weakness passed on from the father to the two sons.

Naomi now determined to return to her homeland, for she had heard that "the Lord had visited his people in giving them bread" (1:6). With the famine no longer existing in Bethlehem, she reasoned that she would fare much better at home with loved ones and friends. As Naomi was some distance on her way back, accompanied by her two daughters-in-law, she told them that they should return to the homes of their own mothers. Both Orpah and Ruth insisted that they wanted to return with her. After considerable entreaty on the part of Naomi, Orpah finally yielded to her mother-in-law's request and returned to her parental home. Ruth, however, refused to leave Naomi. Here recorded in the narrative is the beautiful and stirring declaration of Ruth:

> Entreat me not to leave thee, or to return from following after thee: for whither thou goest, I will go; and where thou lodgest, I will lodge: thy people shall be my people, and thy God my God: Where thou diest, will I die, and there will I be buried: the Lord do so to me, and more also, if ought but death part thee and me. — 1:16, 17.

These beautiful words have been set to lovely music and also are often included in the Christian wedding ceremony.

The two returned to Bethlehem to be welcomed by the people who knew Naomi. It appears that there was great surprise among the women who knew her when once they saw her. They exclaimed, "Is this Naomi?" (1:19). She suggested in her anguish that they should no longer call her Naomi, but Mara, since the Lord had seemed to deal so bitterly with her. It was just at the beginning of the harvest season that Naomi and Ruth had returned.

Chapter 2 begins its account by telling how Ruth asked permission of Naomi to go to the harvest field to glean grain. This was honorable employment and was permitted the poor who might have no other means of support. No doubt it was humiliating especially to Naomi to be so reduced materially that she had nothing. The record indicates that Ruth was supernaturally guided to the fields owned by Boaz, who providentially was also a "kinsman" or relative of the late Elimelech. Here Ruth found favor with the one who was the overseer for Boaz. When Boaz was informed of the identity of the young lady gleaner, he provided additional help for her in the form of water to drink and food to eat, and even charged his field men to leave "handfuls of purpose" of grain for her to glean. He commended her for her devotion to Naomi her mother-in-law, and pronounced the blessing of God upon her for her love and kindness.

When Ruth returned from the fields with an abundance of grain, Naomi was amazed and delighted. Ruth continued to glean in the fields of Boaz all through the harvest season.

In *Chapter 3* there is unfolded an unusual, but completely proper though peculiar, Oriental plan whereby Ruth could make her feelings known to Boaz by taking the position allowed her by the Levirate law. Consequently she "placed herself by night at the feet of Boaz, her kinsman, while he slept." There is no reason to question the purity or honor of either Ruth or Boaz in the execution of this plan, for it was in keeping with the custom of the people of that day and culture. This plan was suggested and put into operation by Naomi, and she waited expectantly to know the outcome of it.

The plan was successful, and in accordance with the customs of that day Boaz accepted the "proposal." However, there was one obstacle that had to be overcome. Boaz realized that there was one other individual who was nearer of kin than he was. If this person wished to perform the kinsman's part, then Boaz would have no rightful claim. But if he did not desire to assume the obligation, then Boaz would have the right.

Chapter 4 reveals that the obligation of the kinsman was to purchase the property that had belonged to the deceased Elimelech, Naomi's husband. This the nearest of kin was willing to do. But along with this obligation was the responsibility of the kinsman to take Ruth as his wife and raise up seed to the deceased. This the nearest of kin did not wish to do. So the way was cleared for Boaz to take Ruth as his wife.

To Boaz and Ruth was born a son who was named Obed. He was the lineal descendant of Judah, the father of Jesse who became the father of David.

"In this book of Ruth may be seen the majestic fulfillment of God's purposes. Even in the dark days of the judges, He was watching over the line through which Christ would come into the world. The genealogy in verses 18-22 discloses that Ruth, the Moabitess, was rewarded for her devotion and loyalty by becoming the great-grandmother of David. The birth of her son was probably not less than forty nor more than one hundred years before the birth of David."[3] It is most significant and a fulfillment of God's plan and purpose that both Boaz and Ruth are mentioned in the Messianic genealogy of Matthew, Chapter 1.

III. THE NATURE OF THE WRITING

The book of Ruth is not written as an historical narrative nor as simple biography. It is more than either of these. In one sense it may be described as a "pastoral," as a picture of rural life — peaceful, simple, and natural. It might also be characterized as presenting a series of pen and ink sketches or idylls in prose, first of the attachment of the young Moabitish widow to Naomi, her desolate mother-in-law, and second, the beautiful reward that in the providence of God, her selfless, sacrificial life was to obtain.

It presents a true story that took place during the period of time when the Judges ruled in Israel. The events described in the book culminate in the revelation of the plan of God to bring to the world a Savior, Jesus Christ. The genealogy with which the book concludes traces the line of the Redeemer through Boaz and Ruth.

The book is also a portrayal of the lives and characters of individuals whose personalities testified to their faith in the divine plan and purpose of God. Their lives were not easy ones, without problems or perplexities, but lives through which God was pleased to operate in carrying out His divine plan.

---

[3] *New Scofield Reference Bible,* Oxford University Press, New York, 1967, p. 321.

Chapter 2

DELIVERANCE FROM DESPAIR (1:1-5)

The late Henry Moorhouse, a noble evangelist, was once passing through some difficult and trying circumstances. He was seeking some word of encouragement from the Lord. One day as he came home his little daughter, who was a paralytic, was sitting in her chair. He brought with him a package for his wife. He kissed his little daughter and said to her, "Where is Mother?" "Mother is upstairs," she replied. "Well, I have a package for her." "Let me carry the package to Mother," said the daughter. "Why, Minnie, dear, how can you carry the package? You cannot carry yourself." With a smile on her face, Minnie said, "Oh no, Father; but you give me the package, and I will carry the package, and you will carry me." Taking her up in his arms, he carried her upstairs, little Minnie and the package too. And then "the word of the Lord came to him" that this was just his position in the work in which he was engaged. He was carrying a burden, but was not God carrying him?

The Old Testament story of Ruth the Moabitess portrays beautifully and tenderly how God carries His trusting saints through apparent defeat and despair to glorious victory and triumph. Let us note the unfolding drama of this true story.

I. DEPRIVATION IN THE FACE OF FAMINE

An honest, sincere, and upright Hebrew of the tribe of Judah, Elimelech by name, lived with the wife of his love and the children of his youth in the vicinity of the city of Bethlehem during the time when the Judges ruled in Israel. As the book of Judges relates, these were days of uncertainty and occasionally of rebellion and anarchy. The record states also that there was a "famine in the land" (1:1). This particular famine might have been caused by a succession of poor crops or it might possibly have resulted from the lack of proper pasture for the domestic animals. Some Bible scholars have suggested that the famine might have occurred at the time described in Judges when the Midianites and the Amalekites "came up with their cattle and their tents, and they came as grasshoppers for multitude; for

17

both they and their camels were without number: and they entered into the land to destroy it. And Israel was greatly impoverished because of the Midianites; and the children of Israel cried unto the Lord" (Judg. 6:5, 6).

As indicated the events that are recorded in the book of Ruth took place "in the days when the judges ruled." These were days of apostasy on the part of God's people. "In those days there was no king in Israel; every man did that which was right in his own eyes" (Judg. 21:25). While the people of Israel had lived in Egypt they had had no self-government since they were slaves under the Pharaohs. When they were set free from the Egyptian bondage and wandered for forty years in the wilderness, Moses ruled them. We read in Deuteronomy 33:5 that "Moses was king in Jeshurun, when the heads of the people and the tribes of Israel were gathered together." When they finally were permitted to enter the land of Canaan, Joshua was their ruler and exercised authority over them. Any one who rebelled against Joshua or would not accept his decrees could be put to death.

"What a difference during the next ensuing period, that of the Judges! It would be hard to find a greater contrast in the history of any people; and that difference came about notwithstanding the fact that, before the death of Joshua, the difficulties of taking possession of the land had been overcome, and the mighty enemies had been conquered, driven from their strong cities, and brought into a state of servitude."[1]

The rule of the Judges was in effect an experiment in an extreme form of democracy. Instead of being great days, they were in contrast very dark days. Here is a lesson for our day. Where there is "no king" and where every one claims his right and his liberty to do "what is right in his own eyes," anarchy will be the inevitable result.

At any rate, Elimelech, through no apparent fault of his own, faced famine and starvation. We believe that he was a God-fearing man. His name means "God is King." His wife's name, Naomi, means "pleasant" or "God is sweet." Some type of action had to be undertaken, and no doubt with God's help and guidance Elimelech determined to move to another country where he might find sustenance for his family.

---

[1] Philip Mauro, *Ruth: The Satisfied Stranger*, p. 21.

II. DETERMINATION IN THE REMOVAL TO MOAB

"They went into the country of Moab and remained there" (1:2). Some have concluded that Elimelech was in error to have left Bethlehem. It is true that he removed his family to an idolatrous country, but there is nothing in the sacred record to suggest that he was to be blamed for his determination to seek a land where there was bread. It is also true that a great deal of misfortune was to befall the family, but let us remember that a man is not to be condemned until there is some definite proof of guilt.

Let us rather suggest that Providence led Elimelech, his wife, and their two sons, into the land of Moab, located on the other side of the Jordan River. Though Bethlehem means "the house of bread" there was no longer sustenance there for Elimelech and his family. Apparently there was a plenteous supply of bread in Moab. Elimelech did not leave Bethlehem because he wanted a better job with higher wages or because he wanted more cultural advantages for his family. He left that he might escape famine and preserve the lives of those who had been entrusted to his care. His action was commendable, and no doubt was the salvation of his family at that particular time in their lives.

A beautiful story is told of how the father of Matthew Henry (who gave us the monumental commentary on the Scriptures) won the hand of his bride. He was a Presbyterian minister; she an only daughter, and the heiress of a considerable fortune. Her father objected to the proposed match. "You see," he said to his daughter, "he may be a prefect gentleman, a brilliant scholar, and an excellent preacher; but he is a stranger, and we do not even know where he comes from!" "True," replied the daughter, with all of the acumen and insight that her great son afterward displayed, "but we know where he is going, and I would like to go with him." And she did.

Shall we not agree that Elimelech knew "where God was going," and that he chose to go with Him? If this was not so, then surely Elimelech went to Moab in the permissive will of God. "They came into the country of Moab, and continued there" (1:2).

III. DESOLATION IN THE LOSS OF LOVED ONES

In the country of Moab the immigrants established a home, and no doubt learned to adjust and reconcile themselves to the new surroundings and varied circumstances of a foreign land. But life was to deal another swift and severe blow to the little family circle. "And Elimelech, Naomi's husband died, and she was left, and her two sons" (1:3). What a sad and pathetic record of great loss and deep sorrow is encompassed in these brief words! The one to whom Naomi had given her heart and upon whom she had learned to depend as her husband and the father of her two sons, was suddenly taken from her.

The lot of a widow is most often one of hardship and trouble. This would be especially true in Naomi's situation as she was poor and far from home, family, and friends.

After the death of her husband a period of time passed during which the two sons grew to young manhood. No mention is made of any of the testings and trials of this period, but we may be certain there were some. Both sons took to themselves wives of the women of Moab whose names were Orpah and Ruth. Ten years went by and then the record states with chilling brevity: "And Mahlon and Chilion died also, both of them; and the woman was bereft of her two sons and her husband" (1:5).

Naomi was called upon to face a double desolation. After ten years of apparent happiness and well-being both sons passed away. Perhaps there was some inherited or constitutional ailment received from the father that brought the death of the sons. Now there were three widows within one household to bear their burdens of grief and loneliness.

"The path became darker and darker. Mahlon means 'pining' and Chilion 'consumption.' Three graves in a strange land! All the laughter and hope that had given Naomi her name of "pleasant' had turned to sadness; she longed to see the dear village of her childhood and early married life, and to drink the water of the well."[2] What is there left worth living for?

IV. DEMONSTRATION OF GOD'S SUSTAINING GRACE

The hand of God that had appeared to be against Naomi was preparing to make "all things work together for good." She did not give up to despair. Her steadfast faith in God was to be rewarded. She would be led to say with the countless saints of all ages who have gone through similar bereavement, "The Lord gave; and the Lord hath taken away; blessed be the name of the Lord" (Job 1:21).

It is through such experiences that the soul is weaned away from earthly things and that Christian fortitude and character

---

[2] F. B. Meyer, *A Devotional Commentary*, Vol. II, p. 41.

are developed. Though the future was hidden from view, Naomi and her two daughters-in-law were yet the object of God's care and providence.

> He giveth more grace when the burdens grow greater,
>   He sendeth more strength when the labors increase;
> To added affliction He addeth His mercy,
>   To multiplied trials, His multiplied peace.
>
> When we have exhausted our store of endurance,
>   When our strength has failed ere the day is half done;
> When we reach the end of our hoarded resources,
>   Our Father's full giving is only begun.
>
> His love has no limit, His grace has no measure,
>   His power no boundary known unto men;
> For out of His infinite riches in Jesus
>   He giveth and giveth and giveth again.
>
> *— Gospel Herald*

There is an old legend of a benevolent king who had his men place a great heavy stone on a certain roadway over which all of his subjects would have to travel. He then hid himself to see who would try to remove the stone. No one stopped to try to remove the stone, but all worked their way around it, loudly blaming the king for not keeping the roadway clear. Finally, a poor peasant farmer on his way to town with a load of vegetables which he hoped to sell in the market place came to the blocked roadway. He laid down his load and with considerable effort and loss of time managed to move the great stone to the side of the roadway. Then, turning to leave he spied a purse which had been under the stone. He opened the purse and found it to be filled with pieces of gold, with a note from the king indicating that it was all to be the property of the one who would remove the stone.

Can we not say that under every cross our King has hidden a blessing? We may turn back or seek to go around the cross, but if we do we are eternal losers. We cannot dodge the cross without dodging God's blessing, and we cannot refuse the cross without endangering our crown. God is watching.

"Then Naomi arose with her daughters-in-law, that she might return from the country of Moab; for she had heard in the country of Moab how the Lord had visited his people in giving them bread" (1:6).

Before too many months would pass, Naomi's sorrow and loss would turn gloriously to joy and rejoicing. (See Ruth 4:16: "And Naomi took the child, and laid him in her bosom, and became nurse unto him.")

Chapter 3

RESOLUTION AND DECISION (1:6-18)

A story is told of a man who had long been gone from his childhood home which had been located in a small rural village. His business had necessitated his traveling around the world. After a great many years of absence, he determined to visit his old home. When he arrived, he found to his dismay that everything had changed. There was not a street, a store, or even a house that he could recognize. Even the location of the fields and the trees seemed different to him. But there was one thing that was just the same. That was the spring of water out of which as a little barefoot, thirsty boy, he used to drink.

The spiritual training of youth in a Christian home, the love of relatives and friends are as a spring of water which never ceases to flow and which will quench the thirst of the weary and troubled soul.

Something of this feeling began to stir in the soul of Naomi, and it made her long to see the home of her earlier days and to drink the water of the well and eat bread in "the house of bread," Bethlehem.

I. A FIRM RESOLUTION (Naomi)

It was not enough that Naomi might begin to think of home and friends. Resolution was needed that would translate her hopes and wishes into action. Word had come from home to her indicating that "the Lord had visited his people in giving them bread" (1:6).

The ties that had most closely bound Naomi to Moab were now broken in the deaths of her husband and two sons. "The land of Moab was now become a melancholy place to her. It is with little pleasure that she can breathe in that air in which her husband and sons had expired; or go on that ground in which they lay buried out of her sight, but not out of her thoughts."[1]

"Then she arose" (1:6). Like the prodigal son of the gospel,

---

[1] Matthew Henry, Commentary, Vol. II, Revell Co., New York.

she not only thought about home, but she resolved to go home. "I will arise and go back. . . ." Her daughters-in-law went with her as she started back to return to the land of Judah.

At a certain juncture in the way, Naomi said to Orpah and Ruth: "Go, return each to your mother's house; the Lord deal kindly with you, as ye have dealt with the dead, and with me" (1:8). The daughters-in-law were dear to Naomi, and it is certain that she was dear to them. A tearful departure was in store for the three lonely widows. With sincere love and deep affection Naomi kissed them, and asked the Lord to grant them rest and peace as she sought to persuade them to return to their homes.

Deep love and devotion were expressed by the daughters-in-law to their mother-in-law as they said to her, "Surely we will return with thee unto thy people" (1:10).

II. A SAD SEPARATION (Orpah)

Naomi once more entreated her daughters-in-law to leave her: "Turn again, my daughters, go your way" (1:12). She endeavored to make these young ladies see that every step they took with her was leading them farther away from their own mothers' homes. She strongly insisted that they would be better off in Moab than to return to Judah with her.

They both continued to express their desire to accompany her, but finally Orpah yielded and tore herself away. Nothing more is heard of her, though no doubt she found rest and peace in her mother's home.

III. A LOYAL DECISION (Ruth)

Ruth refused to yield and "clung to her mother-in-law" (1:14). No criticism could ever be leveled at either of the young widows, for their devotion was a beautiful thing. In fact, Ruth's devotion could well be described as heroic. "And Ruth said, Entreat me not to leave thee, or to turn away from following after thee; for where thou goest, I will go; and where thou lodgest, I will lodge: thy people shall be my people, and thy God, my God. Where thou diest, will I die, and there will I be buried; the Lord do so to me, and more also, if anything but death part thee and me" (1:16, 17).

"This young woman was to be an ancestor of David and in the line of our Lord's descent. Moabite though she was by birth, Ruth was designated for the high honor of introducing a new strain into the Hebrew race, that was to enrich it and through it the world. Indeed, we may almost detect in her noble and beautiful words some anticipation of the Psalms, which have gone singing down the ages. But how stern is the discipline through which those must pass who are called to the highest tasks! The death of her husband in their early married life, the anguish of Naomi, the separation from her own people, the loneliness of a foreign land — these were part of the great price that Ruth paid."[2]

No doubt there was a quality in Naomi's life and suffering that attracted Ruth to the point that she could not leave her. In Naomi's character she realized that there was a witness that was beyond anything that she had ever known or seen in Moab. There must have been a radiance and a beauty in the very countenance of Naomi that made Ruth realize that here was the example of an inward strength and repose that came from her faith and trust in her God. Are we centers of attraction for God so that others may see Him in us?

A Christian sea captain had been instrumental in the salvation of some of the members of his crew. He asked one of the young converts who prior to his conversion had been a rough character to take a Bible to another of the crew members. "No, no, Captain," said the crewman, "he does not need that!" "But why not?" said the Captain. "It won't do him any good." "But why?" persisted the Captain. "Because it is too soon. That is your Bible, and, thank God, it is now my Bible too; but it not his Bible." "What do you mean by that?" asked the Captain. "Why simply that he has another Bible: *You* are his Bible; he is watching you now. As you live Christ, so Christ will be revealed to him."

Ruth had seen reality in Naomi and therefore wanted to remain with her.

---

[2] F. B. Meyer, *op. cit.*, pp. 41, 42.

Chapter 4

BACK TO BETHLEHEM (1:19-22)

"So they two went until they came to Bethlehem." (1:19). As one studies the attitude of Ruth in her insistence to return to Bethlehem with Naomi, it becomes apparent that it was not only her love for her mother-in-law which prompted her decision, but the experience of a new faith which she had come to know through her and which led her to affirm, "Thy God shall be my God." Let us more closely observe the experience of Naomi upon her return to Bethlehem.

I. MANIFESTATION OF SORROW

What a contrast we find in a comparison of Naomi's experience in leaving Bethlehem with her return! "I went out full and the Lord hath brought me home again empty" (1:21). She had left in the full bloom of womanhood with a husband and two sons. Now she was coming back empty. She had gone out with health and youth. Now, she is broken, if not in health, at least in spirit. She seems almost overcome with grief and distress. She has no visible means of support. She is poor and needy.

She was hardly recognizable to her friends. "Is this Naomi? Is that Naomi?" they cried. "The city was moved about them" —moved with compassion and concern.

To His children today, God has not promised always sunny skies. Life at best is real and earnest. Testings and trials are not infrequent for the child of God. But His promise is that those who trust in Him "shall never want any good thing." "As the snows hide flowers even in the Alps, so beneath all our separations and sorrows there are still plants of the Lord: peace, and hope, and joy, and rest in Him. Blessed, indeed, shall we be if we can rest in the Lord, and wait patiently for Him. We, too, shall all change. Time and sorrow will write their experiences on our brow. There will be hours in which we feel like Naomi, empty, oh! so empty. The cup of affection poured out on the ground, the forest without its songsters, the garden without its flowers, the home without its familiar faces. We shall see these pictures every day, and wonder, more and more, how any hearts can do without a Brother and a Savior in Jesus Christ. But if character be enriched and trained, all is well; for this very end have we had Divine discipline, and the Lord will perfect that which concerneth us for the highest ends of eternal life in Him."[1]

II. INTERPRETATON OF PROVIDENCE

As Naomi reviewed the scenes of her earlier years, and looked once again upon the sympathizing friends and neighbors who surrounded her she said, "Call me not Naomi (*pleasant*) but Mara (*bitter*); for the Almighty hath dealt very bitterly with me" (1:20). Who can blame Naomi for giving vent to her feelings of loss and loneliness? In the discouraging and dark circumstances in which she now found herself she might well give way to feelings of despondency.

"The Lord hath testified against me," she declared further to her friends. It is human nature to assume that when God, who could prevent affliction and loss, permits them, that He no longer looks with love and favor upon the afflicted one. But this is a short-sighted view and not a true one! We must not forget that "whom He loveth He chasteneth," and that "the trial of faith is precious."

Naomi stated, "The Lord hath brought me home again empty" (1:21). It is much easier for us to feel that Providence has led us when all has gone well. In fact the word providence as defined in the dictionary is "the care or benevolent guidance of God." But it would be incorrect to limit Providence to only that which is pleasant. We are reminded of the word of the patriarch Job when all he possessed including his family and his property were taken from him, "The Lord gave, and the Lord hath taken away; blessed be the name of the Lord" (Job 1:21).

In all situations and circumstances of life, whether pleasant or adverse, we ought to say with the Psalmist, "Bless the Lord, O my soul, and all that is within me, bless his holy name" (Ps. 103:1).

III. RECOGNITION OF SOVEREIGNTY

Naomi was very soon to see that "all things work together for good to them that love the Lord" (Rom. 8:28). Even the trials that may come through man's immaturity or perhaps through his unwise choices or acts, come to pass by the permissive will

---

[1] Pulpit Commentary, Vol. 8, p. 28.

of God, and are so over-ruled by Him that they result in good to those who love Him. It is so often true as the poet Cowper wrote:

> Behind a frowning Providence
> God hides a smiling face!

Mrs. F. W. Suffield wrote:

God is still on the throne, And He will remember His own;
Though trials may press us and burdens distress us,
He never will leave us alone;
God is still on the throne — He never forsaketh His own;
His promise is true, He will not forget you,
God is still on the throne.

Sudden changes in our plans may sometimes be hard to accept. Sometimes they are forced upon us by circumstances over which we have no control. God sees us and plans our ways and guides us accordingly. That is why He may permit reverses and failures to come our way. He sometimes changes our plans, for He sees the danger in them. What a blessing then that God does not always let us carry out our plans! Knowing the end from the beginning He makes no mistakes.

The late James M. Gray wrote, "Once, when convalescing from a long illness, it was suggested that for the benefit of the change I visit the British provinces. The arrangements were all made when unexpectedly another malady threw me back on my bed again. How disappointing! For what was I waiting longer in the sick room? Soon I received a satisfactory answer. Picking up a newspaper one day, I read that the steamer on which I should have sailed struck a reef on entering St. John Harbor and almost instantly sank."

> Behind our lives the Weaver stands,
> And works His wondrous will;
> We leave it in His all-wise hands,
> And trust His perfect skill.

There is such a thing as divine government of human affairs. God is on the throne and He does direct the affairs of men and nations. The late Wm. L. Pettingill, well-known Bible teacher and author of many books, made a penetrating remark about the will of God: "Most people," he said, "don't want to know the will of God in order to do it; they want to know it in order just to *consider* it."

J. R. Miller writes: "God's will is always the best; it is always divine love. A stricken wife, standing beside the coffin of her husband, said to a friend: 'There lies my husband, my only earthly support, my most faithful human friend, one who has never once failed me; but I must not forget that there lies also the will of God, and that will is perfect love.' By faith she saw good and the blessing in what appeared to her the wreck of all her happiness. But truly the good and the blessing are in every dark providence which comes into the life of God's child. Our Father never means us harm in anything He does or permits.[2]

---

[2] Walter B. Knight, *Illustrations for Christian Service*, Wm. B. Eerdmans Publishing Co., 1949, p. 722.

Chapter 5

HANDFULS ON PURPOSE (2:1-17)

In his book, *Ruth the Redeemed,* the late Arthur Petrie tells this story: "When Sir Thomas Lipton of England was a restaurateur, he devised an ingenious way to advertise his restaurant. He equipped six tall, thin men with sandwich boards and sent them around town. On the sandwich boards were the words: 'Going to Lipton's.' Of course people read the legend, and no doubt felt that the thin men needed a good meal at Lipton's. Some weeks later he fitted out six tall stout men, and sent them around town. On the sandwich boards they carried were the words: 'Coming from Lipton's.'" Dr. Petrie added, "We, like Ruth, come to the Lord as poor, helpless strangers. We go into His field where there is plenty of spiritual food; we should be a testimony to others that we have gleaned from Him. We should reflect His goodness to us."

In the second chapter of the book of Ruth we find beautifully illustrated the Mosaic provision for helping those in material need. As explained in Leviticus 19:9, 10 and in Deuteronomy 24:19 the law permitted those who were poor, or who were strangers, or were fatherless, or were widows, to "glean" in the fields. This simply gave them the right and privilege to follow the harvesters in the fields and to pick up whatever had been left of the grain. Ruth met these requirements since she was a foreigner, was a widow, and was poor. No doubt Naomi had explained these provisions to Ruth who was now eager to try her skill in the fields as a gleaner.

I. THE HARVEST FIELD

The area surrounding Bethlehem, "the house of bread," was noted for its fertile valleys and rich pastures. Bethlehem is a town in the hill country of Judah and is located about five miles south of Jerusalem. In the vicinity of Bethlehem are vineyards and orchards of fig and olive trees. Though the fields are some-

---

1 *Ruth the Redeemed,* Fourth Edition, Seattle, Washington.

what stony, they nonetheless produce an abundance of grain. Even today there is gleaning to be seen in some of the fields, as in the day of Ruth and Naomi.

As a village Bethlehem existed as early as the time of Jacob. The first reference in the Bible to Bethlehem is in Genesis 35:19 where we read of the death of Rachel, Jacob's wife, in childbirth (Benjamin) at Bethlehem. As the birthplace and ancestral home of David, the town became known as the city of David (cf. Luke 2:11). Some seven hundred years or more before the birth of Christ, the prophet Micah proclaimed, "But thou, Bethlehem Ephrathah, though thou be little among the thousands of Judah, yet out of thee shall he come forth unto me that is to be ruler in Israel, whose goings forth have been from of old, from everlasting" (Micah 5:2).

Another interesting Scripture having to do with the vicinity of Bethlehem relates the annunciation, to the shepherds on the hillsides "keeping watch over their flocks by night," of Christ's birth in the town (cf. Luke 2:8).

"A little east of the town is the church built by Helena, the mother of Constantine, over the cave said to be the stable in which the nativity took place. Half a mile to the north of the town is the traditional tomb of Rachel. On the southern side of the town is a valley running to the Dead Sea."[2] So much for the geography and early history of Bethlehem.

Naomi and Ruth came to Bethlehem at "the beginning of barley harvest" (1:22). It was not the custom in Palestine to separate the fields of corn or other grain by walls and hedges, but only by the use of a furrow with a small collection of stones, or sometimes by single stones placed upright at distances of a rod or more from each other.

The field in which Ruth went to glean was one of the fields belonging to Boaz. The record states: "She happened to come to a portion of the field belonging unto Boaz, who was of the kindred of Elimelech" (2:3).

II. THE HARVESTER (Ruth)

"Let me now go to the field, and glean ears of grain" (2:2). The harvest season of ancient Palestine was divided into two periods of time. Barley harvest preceded the wheat harvest by about two weeks. The beginning of the harvest season was con-

---

2 John D. Davis, *A Dictionary of the Bible,* pp. 90, 91.

secrated by the bringing of the sheaf of the firstfruits. "When ye are come into the land which I give unto you, and shall reap the harvest thereof, then ye shall bring a sheaf of the first fruits of your harvest unto the priest" (Lev. 23:10).

Harvest began in the lowlands before the crops were ripe on the hills. In the hot Jordan Valley, barley harvest commenced in April, when the Jordan was full at the close of the rainy season. Wheat harvest lingered in the uplands to the month of June. When the harvest was completed, and the produce gathered in, there were great rejoicings. The feasts of unleavened bread, of weeks or harvest, and of ingathering, all had a relation to the season of reaping.

The harvest time was always a time of joy and rejoicing. The one who came on the scene at the beginning of the harvest time was then ready to partake of the joy and blessings of the entire harvest.

Ruth did not hesitate to stoop to very lowly work. As has been indicated, only the very poor would be found in the fields gleaning after the harvesters. Ruth was willing to humble herself, and in this we find rich instruction and helpful example.

The saintly Andrew Murray once wrote: "The highest lesson a believer has to learn is humility. Oh, that every Christian who seeks to advance in a holy life may remember this well! Humility isn't thinking meanly of oneself — it isn't thinking of oneself at all. The truly humble man does not know that he is humble: Moses knew not that the face of his skin shone!"

A party of English tourists visited the house where Beethoven, the great composer, had spent the last years of his life. The caretaker (who was something of a hero worshipper) led them at length into a certain room, and reverently lifting the cover, said, "And this was Beethoven's piano." A young lady of the party at once took possession of the music stool and began to play one of Beethoven's sonatas. The custodian stood by, stern and silent. At last the young lady swung around on her stool and said, "I suppose a great many people who come here like to play on Beethoven's piano?" "Well, miss," said the caretaker, "Paderewski was here last summer, and some of his friends wanted him to play, but he said, "No, I am not worthy to play on Beethoven's piano."

When someone asked Saint Francis of Assisi why and how he could accomplish so much, he replied: "This may be why. The Lord looked down from heaven upon the earth and said, 'Where can I find the weakest, the littlest, the poorest man on the face of the earth?' Then He saw me and said, 'Now I've found him, and will work through him. He won't be proud of it. He'll see that I am only using him because of his littleness and insignificance.'"

Ruth evidenced real courtesy and concern for her mother-in-law in securing her approval to glean in the fields. "Let me now go to the field and glean . . ." (2:2). Doubtless, it was not easy for Naomi to let her go. "Has it come to this?" she must have thought. "Are we so reduced in circumstances that we must glean in the fields?"

The loving Father in heaven was leading Ruth in a path that she could never even have imagined. She was led by God until she came to a field that was owned by Elimelech's kinsman, Boaz. Though the sacred record says that she "happened to come to a portion of the fields belonging to Boaz" (2:3) it does not mean that this was entirely by chance. Though outwardly it might seem a coincidence, we may be certain that she was led of Providence. She went to work with a will and a purpose as she "gleaned in the field after the reapers" (2:3).

III. THE HUSBANDMAN (Boaz)

Boaz came from Bethlehem to inspect the work being done by his crew of harvesters. He was on friendly terms with his workmen and took a keen interest in them and in their labors. He exchanged the customary greetings with his men and added the Hebrew blessing, "The Lord be with you" (2:4). This kind consideration evoked a similar reply from his men, "The Lord bless thee" (2:4).

As Boaz looked more closely at his fields he became immediately aware of one whom he had not seen there before — a beautiful young lady. He called to his steward or foreman and inquired, "Whose damsel is this?" (2:5). The servant then explained that she was the Moabitish daughter-in-law of Naomi. Along with his answer the steward volunteered other information of a highly complimentary nature concerning her and her diligence and industry. She had respectfully requested permission to glean. She had worked very diligently all morning. She didn't take any time off for resting.

Boaz then went immediately to her, greeted her cordially and told her that she was to remain in his fields to glean. He also instructed the young men to respect her, and suggested that she was to refresh herself at his expense when she would become thirsty.

With real respect and reverence Ruth bowed before Boaz, asking him how it could be that he would take knowledge of her, a foreigner. Boaz then commended Ruth for her kind and considerate care of Naomi and indicated to her that it pleased him to show kindness to her. "And Boaz answered and said unto her, It hath fully been shown me, all that thou hast done for thy mother-in-law since the death of thine husband, and how thou hast left thy father and thy mother, and the land of thy nativity, and art come unto a people whom thou knewest not heretofore. The Lord recompense thy work, and a full reward be given thee by the Lord God of Israel, under whose wings thou art come to trust" (2:11, 12).

Ruth was also invited by Boaz to join them at meal time, and to partake of the food prepared for his workmen. When she returned to the fields following the noon hour, she discovered that Boaz had instructed his men to let her glean among the sheaves and to "let fall also some of the handfuls of purpose for her" (2:16). When Ruth "beat out what she had gleaned" at the end of the day it amounted to about an ephah (three pecks and five quarts).

An unforeseen development is beginning to unfold, and we note how the heart of Boaz has been captured by the young lady. The evidence of the blessing of God upon her caused her to gain favor with Boaz. In the providence of God this selfless young lady was to receive the reward of heaven.

The Word of God tells us that "God setteth the solitary in families" (Ps. 68:6). Human love that is blessed and sanctified by the love of Christ makes life worth living. God ordained that the man "should cleave unto his wife, and that the two should become one flesh." There is historical and empirical evidence that the family is here to stay, despite the predictions of some pseudo-prophets of our day who say that the family unit is "old-fashioned," and "on the way out." Our personal lives revolve around our family groups.

There is more to love than romance and infatuation. Every human being has two basic emotional needs. He has a need for love and for significance. "True love holds fast through hardship and sorrow; it is man's greatest source of joy and strength; and when we love truly, we come closest to expressing in human nature that which is like to divine."[3]

---

[3] Wynona Farquhar Leonard, *Love that Lasts a Lifetime*, p. 10.

The Hebrew and Christian concepts of love are in sharp contrast to the secular and erotic emphases of love that is only physical. The Scriptures exalt the role of womanhood. In the home she is the "queen" who fills it with the charm of her quiet influence. "The heart of her husband doth safely trust in her. Her children rise up, and call her blessed; her husband also, and he praiseth her" (Prov. 31:11, 28).

The hand of God was upon Ruth and Boaz to bring them together in His perfect plan and for His divine purpose.

Chapter 6

HARVEST HAPPENINGS (2:18-23)

A story is told of an engineer who was confined to his bed, his lower limbs being paralyzed through a serious accident. Because of his reputation for great skill he was asked to design and prepare the blueprints for a great suspension bridge. After many months his plans were completed and placed in the hands of those who were to be in charge of the construction of the bridge. After many more months the bridge construction was completed. The engineer was brought on his bed to the scene of the beautiful bridge spanning the wide river. As he watched for the first time the cars speed over the bridge and looked at the blueprints which he held in his hands, the tears began to fill his eyes, and he cried out, "It's just like the plan; it's just like the plan."

Certain it is that God has blueprints for our lives. The question we must ask ourselves is whether or not we have found His plan for our lives and if we are walking according to His will. There could be no greater reward, when looking back over our lives from eternity, than to be able to hear Him say, "It's just like the plan; it's just like the plan."

Let us note in these closing verses of Ruth, Chapter 2, how God's perfect plan is progressing toward fulfillment for Naomi and Ruth. Picture the scene as the setting of the sun prepares the way for the curtains of night to be drawn over and around the little town of Bethlehem. "Oh little town of Bethlehem, how still we see thee lie." Naomi is anxiously looking for the return of Ruth after her day of gleaning in the fields. Ruth is slowly wending her way homeward with her heavy burden of grain, to the humble abode which she shares with Naomi. She is weary from the day's toil, but is no doubt rejoicing in the day's good fortune and eager to share her success with her mother-in-law.

I. BESTOWAL

"And she took it up and went into the city. And her mother-in-law saw what she had gleaned" (2:18). With a real sense of gratitude, and even with some pride perhaps, Ruth deposited her heavy burden at the feet of Naomi, her mother-in-law. Apparently she also gave her mother-in-law the remainder of the lunch that had been given to her by the reapers out in the field: "She brought out and gave to her what she had reserved [left over] after she was satisfied" (2:18).

Naomi was so excited and grateful for the overflowing evidence of the bountiful gleaning in the harvest that she exclaimed, "Where did you glean today and where did you work?" (2:19). She could tell from the size of the load of grain and from the beaming countenance of Ruth that the day's work had brought unmeasured blessing. "All of that? What a wonderful gleaner you are!"

Ruth explained to Naomi where she had worked and said, "The man's name with whom I worked today is Boaz" (2:19). What a thrill must have come to Naomi as she heard once again that familiar and beneficent name!

II. BLESSING

"And Naomi said unto her daughter-in-law, Blessed be he of the Lord who hath not withheld his kindness to the living and to the dead" (2:20). Naomi had not lost sight of the family connections of her late husband, and when the name of Boaz was mentioned she remembered it and recognized it as one of Elimelech's nearest of kindred.

The recollection of his kindness and concern came anew to her mind. Here was evidence that he was still a generous and a gracious relative. No doubt the name and deeds of Boaz were the theme of the conversation carried on between the two women that evening. Ruth related to Naomi how Boaz had told her to stay in his fields until the harvest was completed (2:21). Naomi then encouraged her to do just that and not to go to any other fields. "And if one could have read the hearts of both, as at length they laid themselves down to rest, perhaps the thoughts of each might have been found to be running in the strain of the words of a great descendant, as he said and sang, 'Thou hast put gladness in my heart, more than in the time that their corn and their wine increased. I will both lay me down in peace, and sleep: for thou, Lord, only makest me dwell in safety.' "[1]

III. BENEFIT

"So Ruth kept close by the maidens of Boaz to glean until the

---

[1] Pulpit Commentary, *op. cit.*, p. 45.

end of barley harvest and of wheat harvest, and dwelt with her mother-in-law" (2:23). We may be certain that the harvest season brought rich reward to Ruth and Naomi by the time it was over. They no doubt received sufficient to take care of their needs and to help to establish them again as citizens of Bethlehem.

The bountiful harvest yield witnessed to the mercy and goodness of God to His trusting servants. His promise to all of mankind that "seed time and harvest shall not cease" was again fulfilled. He daily "loadeth us with benefits." "Surely goodness and mercy shall follow us all the days of our lives."

Charles H. Spurgeon, the prince of English preachers, told how he once laughed when preparing a sermon, the only time he ever remembered having laughed in so serious a business. He was going to preach a sermon about Joseph, but it seemed that wherever Spurgeon began he always made a short cut to Christ, and he quickly did it this time. He had drawn a picture of the colossal stores of corn in Egypt. The granaries were bursting with abundance — a supply of corn to last for the seven years of famine. Then in the midst of this vivid conception of such great plenty and abundance, Spurgeon imagined that he saw a little mouse over in one corner of a granary. What do you suppose that little mouse was doing? He was worrying himself to death — nothing but skin and bones were left — in the fear that there wasn't going to be enough for him to live on. This made Spurgeon laugh to imagine such a fantastic picture of insecurity.

But aren't a lot of Christians like the little mouse? God is our Father and Christ is our Savior, and the wealth of heaven and earth is at our disposal, and yet we sometimes worry that there won't be enough.

Ruth and Naomi blessed the Lord for His bountiful provision for them.

> Praise the Lord for He is glorious:
> Never shall His promise fail;
> God hath made His saints victorious;
> Sin and death shall not prevail.
>
> Praise the God of our salvation;
> Hosts on high His power proclaim;
> Heaven and earth and all creation
> Laud and magnify His name.

Chapter 7

STEPS TO REST (3:1-18)

At thirty-two years of age, William Cowper passed through a great crisis in his life. In despondency, he tried more than once to take his own life. Then one morning, in a moment of strange cheerfulness, he took up his Bible and read a verse from the book of Romans. In a moment he received strength to believe, and rejoiced in the forgiving power of God. Some years later, after he had passed through a rich Christian experience and had written many beautiful hymns, he sat and meditated on God's dealings with him, and with others. This led to the writing of his great hymn concerning divine providence:

> God moves in a mysterious way
> His wonders to perform;
> He plants His footsteps in the sea,
> And rides upon the storm.
>
> Deep in unfathomable mines
> Of never-failing skill,
> He treasures up His bright designs,
> And works His sovereign will.

Let us now observe a further step in the providence of God at work in the lives of Naomi and Ruth to bring about the fulfillment of His divine will for their future.

I. NAOMI'S PROGRAM

"Then Naomi, her mother-in-law, said unto her, My daughter, shall I not seek rest for thee, that it may be well with thee?" (3:1). It is quite apparent from what follows in the chapter that the "rest" which Naomi had in mind was to be found for Ruth in a home of her own with a husband to love her and care for her. This was the "rest" of having one to spend his life with you, and to be able to rest in his love and in his care. Perhaps Naomi had observed following the conclusion of the harvest season, that Ruth seemed unusually sad and lonely. The outdoor activity of her strenuous work had kept her busy and occupied. Now she

was perhaps spending most of her time indoors, and so could
be the subject of close observation on the part of her mother-in-
law. Perhaps also Naomi had noticed the more than ordinary
attention which Boaz had given Ruth. She determined to do
something about it.

In seeking a husband for Ruth, Naomi decided to follow the
custom of the country and the culture of that day. Hence she
proposed to Ruth the carrying out of a procedure that was per-
missible and proper according to the Levirate law. It was apparently a time-honored custom which was in force among the
Hebrews. Consequently she instructed Ruth in the exact method
that was to be followed in her "proposal" to Boaz.

II. RUTH'S PROPOSAL

The Levirate Law was "a law that gave a widow, if an heiress,
the right to claim from the nearest of kin to her deceased husband, conjugal assistance in the management of her estate." The
nearest of kin, if thus appealed to for the purpose indicated,
had a right to refuse or to accept the widow's claim. There were
specific regulations outlined to be followed in perpetuating the
name of a deceased relative (Deut. 24:5-10).

In other words, this was the prescribed way of informing a
kinsman that not only was it his right, but that also this was a
request to him that he should institute the necessary legal steps
to carry out his responsibility. Accordingly, Ruth made the
necessary preparation by washing, anointing herself and putting
on beautiful raiment. She then "placed herself by night at the
feet of Boaz while he slept," and the proposal was consummated.

Let us clearly observe again that there was no indication of
immodesty or immorality in Ruth's proposal. It was carried out
in conformity with the prevailing and accepted custom of the
day. Likewise Boaz's action showed his concern to retain un-
tarnished and honorable his own unsullied reputation.

III. BOAZ'S PROTECTION

Boaz acted with admirable self-restraint. His genuine concern
was for the good name of this young lady who had placed herself at his disposal to seek his protection. He was most desirous
of protecting and guarding the name and reputation of Ruth.
The record indicates that though Boaz was most ready and willing to accept Ruth's proposal, he knew that there was one other
individual who was a near kinsman (closer relative) than he

himself. This person he knew by all legal rights was entitled to receive the first offer.

We may wonder at the gift of six measures of barley that Boaz gave to Ruth when she rose up to leave him in the morning. As a present from one so wealthy as Boaz it would appear to be a rather inconsequential gift. However, further observation and understanding of his action would lead us to realize that the gift was perhaps most suitable. Boaz wanted to give evidence of his sympathy, concern, and protection to Ruth, but honorable man that he was, he did not feel that at this point in his dealings with her he could give her an unqualified answer to her proposal. He knew that he must make arrangements for the nearest of kin to have the first choice of Ruth.

Ruth returned to Naomi and reported the result of her proposal to Boaz. She showed the gift of barley and stated that Boaz had not wanted her to return empty-handed to her mother-in-law. Naomi advised Ruth to "sit still until thou know how the matter will fall; for the man will not rest, until he have finished the thing this day" (3:18).

This was as though Naomi were saying to Ruth, "Don't worry. Be at peace. All is going to work out as God directs." We are once again reminded that "all things work together for good to them that love the Lord and are the called according to his purpose" (Rom. 8:28). Chapter 4 of the book reveals the truth of this.

James H. McConkey once said, "God has a plan for every life. What a wondrous truth this is! And yet how reasonable a one. Shall the architect draw the plans for his stately palace? Shall the artist sketch the outlines of his masterpiece? Shall the shipbuilder lay down the lines for his colossal ship? And yet shall God have no plan for the soul which He brings into being and puts 'in Christ Jesus?' Surely He has."

"Yea, for every cloud that floats across the summer sky: for every blade of grass that points its tiny spear Heavenward, God has a purpose and a plan. How much more then, for you who are His own in Christ Jesus, does God have a perfect life plan."

Chapter 8

THE CHRONOLOGY OF CHRIST (4:1-22)

When William Jennings Bryan went to call on the father of his prospective wife to seek the hand of his daughter in marriage, knowing the strong religious feeling of the father, he thought to strengthen his case by a quotation from the Bible. He quoted the proverb of Solomon: "Whoso findeth a wife findeth a good thing" (Prov. 18:22). To his surprise the father replied with a citation from the Apostle Paul to the effect that he that marrieth doeth well, but that he that marrieth not doeth better. The young suitor was for a moment confused. Then with a happy inspiration he replied that Paul had had no wife and Solomon had had seven hundred, and Solomon, therefore, ought to be the better judge as to marriage.

Chapter 4 of the book of Ruth tells the beautiful story of the culmination of the years of struggle and toil of Naomi and Ruth. Only the hand of God could have directed them to such happy circumstances after the sorrow and loss of their earlier years. Let us note in detail the unfolding drama of the concluding chapter of the book.

I. THE MARRIAGE CONSUMMATED

Before the marriage of Ruth and Boaz could take place there was one obstacle that had to be overcome. This obstacle was not on the part of either Boaz or Ruth. Boaz's heart was by now captivated with Ruth. There was no hindrance either in his financial circumstances nor in his physical condition apparently. And Ruth had already declared her willingness to become Boaz's wife.

As indicated in the previous chapter, the obstacle or hindrance was a technical one that hinged on the obligation of a certain law. "Two Old Testament laws are involved in this story (vv. 3-5). The law regulating redemption of property ('the parcel of land, which was Elimelech's' vs. 3) is given in Leviticus 25:25-34. The law concerning a brother's duty to raise up seed to the deceased, the Levirate Law, is given in Deuteronomy 25:5-10: 'If brethren dwell together, and one of them die, and have no child, the wife of the dead shall not marry outside the family unto a stranger; her husband's brother shall go in unto her, and take her to him as his wife, and perform the duty of an husband's brother unto her. And it shall be, that the first-born whom she beareth shall succeed in the name of his brother who is dead, that his name be not put out of Israel. And if the man desire not to take his brother's wife, then let his brother's wife go up to the gate unto the elders, and say, My husband's brother refuseth to raise up unto his brother a name in Israel; he will not perform the duty of my husband's brother. Then the elders of his city shall call him, and speak unto him; and if he stand to it, and say, I desire not to take her, Then shall his brother's wife come unto him in the presence of the elders, and loose his shoe from off his foot, and spit in his face, and shall answer and say, So shall it be done unto that man who will not build up his brother's house. And his name shall be called in Israel, The house of him who hath his shoe loosed.' The word 'brother' is capable of extended interpretation (cf. Lev. 25:48-49; Judg. 9:3)."[1]

Boaz was most desirous of bringing to a decision the important matter of the "next of kin's" obligation and relationship to Ruth. Hence, he made haste to go to the city-gate which was not only the principal place of concourse or assemblage for the residents of the town, but also served as a kind of legislative town hall. It was here that all legal matters were heard and decisions rendered.

When the citizens had gathered together including the one who was the nearest of kin (to Ruth), Boaz lost no time in presenting the problem. Naomi, because of being in reduced circumstances had resolved to sell the property which had belonged to her deceased husband Elimelech. Boaz now offered the property to the next of kin who indicated his desire to purchase it. Then Boaz added that it would also be required by the law that the nearest of kin would take Ruth to be his wife. When he heard this, the nearest of kin withdrew his offer and suggested that Boaz should have all legal rights.

To fulfill the legal aspect of the agreement the nearest of kin then removed his shoe and gave it to Boaz in testimony of the fact that he was surrendering all of his rights to both the property and to Ruth.

The removal of the shoe was a symbolic custom or gesture in

---

[1] *New Scofield Reference Bible,* New York, 1967, p. 320.

Israel relating to the selling and the buying of land and of acquiring or surrendering rights of kinship (cf. 4:7.)

With the legal aspect completed and witnessed by the "elders" and God's blessing pronounced upon the plans for marriage, all was now in readiness for the consummation of the wedding. "So Boaz took Ruth and she was his wife" (4:13). The blessing which "makes rich and to which no sorrow is added," the blessing of God, attended the union.

The late Clarence E. Macartney, Presbyterian minister, has written these beautiful words concerning marriage: "Rebekah said, 'I will go' (Gen. 24:58). How that answer has echoed upon the lips of thousands and thousands of the sisters of Rebekah! 'Wilt thou go?' and back has come the answer, 'I will go' — earth's sweetest music, no doubt, to those who hear both sentences! 'I will go!' And she has gone — although it meant the crossing of broad seas; a hut in a land of savages; a rude frontier settlement; one room in the third story back, which must serve as bedroom, living room, and kitchen. 'I will go!' And she has gone — although it has meant separation, loneliness, childbearing, sickness, grief, sometimes disappointments, sorrow, and tragedy. Yet the world keeps on going, because men ask, 'Wilt thou go?' and women still answer with radiant eye and tremulous voice, 'I will go.' "[2]

We see in the consummation of the marriage of Ruth and Boaz, the actual fulfillment of the promise that Ruth had made to Naomi when she left her own home and parents in Moab to go with Naomi to Bethlehem: "Where thou goest, I will go; and where thou lodgest, I will lodge: thy people shall be my people, and thy God, my God" (1:16). This clear statement indicated the firm resolve of Ruth to cast her lot forever with the family of her mother-in-law Naomi. It is a beautiful example for all of the "daughters" of Ruth to emulate.

Ruth and Boaz became "one flesh" in a union that was to fulfill the purpose and plan of God in the redemption of all mankind.

II. THE BIRTH CELEBRATED

What a remarkable and exciting event is announced in the beautiful words, "And Ruth bore a son" (4:13). The women, neighbors of Naomi announced the blessed event, saying, "There

---

[2] From *Macartney's Illustrations*, by Clarence E. Macartney. Copyright 1945 by Whitmore and Stone. Used by permission of Abingdon Press, p. 224.

is a son born to Naomi; and they called his name Obed: he is
the father of Jesse, the father of David" (4:17). This is a striking
statement made by the women: "There is a son born to Naomi."
He was to be to Naomi "a restorer of thy life, and a nourisher
of thine old age" (4:15). The birth of Obed was the culmination
of all of Naomi's hopes and dreams down through the years of
her sorrow and deep loss. The name Obed means "servant." He
is a type of Christ, the servant of Jehovah.

What a great blessing from God is the birth of a little child!
What possibilities and potentials for God and for good are
wrapped up in a little child! How true is the word of Christ
when He said, "Of such is the kingdom of heaven." "A little child
shall lead them!"

Little Obed brought great blessing to his mother, his father,
and his grandmother. Ruth would think of Mahlon and would
rejoice. Naomi would rejoice as she thought of her husband
Elimelech. Boaz would rejoice in the birth of Obed as he thought
of both of the deceased. Ruth would thank God that Boaz had a
son, and Boaz would be grateful to know that Ruth and Naomi's
fondest hopes and dreams had been realized in the coming of
the "little gift" from heaven. Naomi would no longer want her
name to be changed from "pleasant" to "bitter." God had honored her faith and her faithfulness and her name was again
Naomi.

We may be certain that Obed would live up to his name,
"servant." He would fulfill this designation to his grandmother,
mother, and father. And above all, he would have a ministry to
fulfill to the Heavenly Father as he was to be a "link" in the
coming of the promised Messiah into the dark world.

> When little boys kneel by their beds
> And fold their hands and bow their heads
> And shut their eyes and start to pray
> I don't think God is far away.
> I think He listens with intent
> To any message that is sent
> By little boys who kneel at night;
> I think God tries with all His might
> To answer prayers that small boys make
> In His Son's name, for His Son's sake.
> — Gates Hebbard

We may be certain that in this godly home it was "line upon
line and precept upon precept" for little Obed to follow. And

God was there to hear his prayer and to bless and direct his life.

What a powerful example Obed's great Descendant set for us in His relationship to children! "Then some little children were brought to him, so that he could put his hands on them and pray for them. The disciples frowned on the parent's action but Jesus said, 'You must let little children come to me, and you must never stop them. The Kingdom of heaven is made of little children like them!' Then he laid his hands on them and went his way" (Matt. 19:13, 14, Phillips). On another occasion the Lord called a little child to him and set him in the midst of his ambitious disciples and said, Except ye be converted, and become as little children, ye shall not enter the kingdom of heaven" (Matt. 18:2, 3).

"How can I bring up my son in the way he should go?" asked an anxious father. "By going that way yourself," was the reply. This reminds us that words are quite easily forgotten, but the example of a good life makes a lasting impression. "Train up a child in the way he should go, and, when he is old, he will not depart from it" (Prov. 22:6).

"There is a stately simplicity in the story of the issue: 'They called his name Obed: he is the father of Jesse, the father of David.' In this final word of the book there is manifest the Divine movement in the history of the chosen people. Thus the kingly line was ordered in the midst of infidelity, through faithful souls. Presently the people clamored for a king, and one was appointed for a time, through whom they learned the difference between earthly rule and the direct government of God. The man after God's own heart succeeded him, and his coming was from those who had realized the Divine ideal, and walked humbly with God. Yet a larger issue followed as the centuries passed. From this union came at last, as to the flesh, Jesus the Christ."[3]

III. THE LINEAGE CERTIFIED

"And Obed begot Jesse, and Jesse begot David" (4:22).

"The book of the genealogy of Jesus Christ, the son of David, the son of Abraham. And Salmon begot Boaz of Rahab; and Boaz begot Obed of Ruth; and Obed begot Jesse; and Jesse begot David, the king. . . . And Jacob begot Joseph, the husband of Mary, of whom was born Jesus, who is called Christ. So all

---

[3] From *The Analyzed Bible* by G. Campbell Morgan. Copyright 1959 by Fleming H. Revell Company. All rights reserved, p. 83.

the generations from Abraham to David are fourteen generations; and from David until the carrying away into Babylon are fourteen generations; and from the carrying away into Babylon unto Christ are fourteen generations" (Matt. 1:1, 5, 6, 16, 17).

A street preacher in London many years ago was preaching to a crowd that had gathered around him. It was at the time of the Shamrock Races, and everyone was talking about the event. A ruffian on the edge of the crowd desiring to have a little fun called out, "Mr. Preacher! What do you know about the Shamrock?" The preacher continued his preaching. A second time the disturber called out, "I say, Mr. Preacher, what do you know about the Shamrock?" Still the speaker paid no heed, but preached on. Finally, a third time, not to be silenced, the heckler called out, "Mr. Preacher! I am asking you what you know about the Shamrock!" This time the preacher paused. The crowd became very still. Pointing upward with one hand, he said, so clearly and distinctily that all could hear him, "On Christ, the Solid Rock I stand; all other rocks are — shamrocks!"

Let us not forget that Christ is indeed the Rock of Ages, the very foundation of our faith.

Our final concern is with some lessons that come to us in the words of Ruth 4:22 as they are related to Matthew 1:1-17. Here we find recorded the "Chronology of Christ," the "book of the generation of Jesus Christ, the son of David, the son of Abraham." In these verses in Matthew's Gospel are sixteen verses of names in which are traced the genealogy of Christ from Abraham to David, and from David to Christ — forty-two generations in all.

Bishop J. C. Ryle in his *Expository Thoughts* says: "Let no one think that these verses are useless. Nothing is useless in creation. Nothing is useless in the Bible. Every word of it is inspired. The chapters and verses which seem at first unprofitable, are all given for some good purpose."[4] With this word we heartily agree and shall endeavor to discover the useful instruction from this chronology.

There are three important teachings that come to us as we study this chronology and see Christ's lineage certified.

The first is that *God is truthful.* One day a little child came to his mother and said, "Mother, who made God?" This mother's face expressed astonishment and chagrin, and she answered

---

[4] *Matthew,* p. 3.

curtly, "What an awful question to ask. You had better run off and play." In the same neighborhood another lad asked his mother, "Did God make Himself?" This mother breathed a silent prayer for wisdom in answering the question. Taking off her wedding band she handed it to her little son and asked, "Where does this ring begin and where does it end?" The boy studied it for a moment and then replied, "There is no starting place and no stopping place to a ring." And the mother wisely replied, "Just so with God. There is no starting or stopping place with Him. He always has been and always will be."

Away back in human history, this God who was from the beginning, called Abraham out from the land of his kindred and told him to go to the land of Canaan. God promised him: "In thee shall all families of the earth be blessed" (Gen. 12:3). In the book of Ruth we read "And Boaz begot Obed, And Obed begot Jesse, and Jesse begot David" (4:21, 22). And in Isaiah 11:1 the record indicates that God promised to raise up a Savior of the family of David: "And there shall come forth a rod out of the stem of Jesse, and a Branch shall grow out of his roots." The sixteen verses of Matthew 1 show that Jesus was the son of David and the son of Abraham; that this was the kingly line in which Christ was to be born. The significance of this is that God keeps His Word — His promises are fulfilled. God's promises are "yea and amen in Christ Jesus."

A young man, a theological student in a certain school, went to visit his aged grandmother during his vacation. He said to her, "Grandmother, you know the Bible that you say you believe was written in the Hebrew and Greek languages. It had to be translated by great scholars into our language. How do you know that those who translated it got it right?"

"Ah, Jamie lad," she answered, "never mind the great men; I have translated a few of those promises myself."

If it is a precious fact for the believer that God is truthful, that He always keeps His word, it is also a solemn fact for the unbeliever. God's Word says, "If ye repent not, ye shall likewise perish." But no one needs to perish, for God has provided a way of salvation through His Son. "The gift of God is eternal life."

The second teaching from these verses is that while God is truthful, *man is sinful.* A closer look at the list of names indicates the wickedness and corruption of mankind. Roboam (Rehoboam), Joram (Jehoram), Amon, and Jechonias (Jehoiakim), all had pious and godly fathers, but they themselves were wicked men and ungodly rulers. They speak to us of the sinfulness of man, and indicate that grace does not necessarily run in families. In other words, it takes something more than good examples and good advice to make children of God. The Apostle John tells us in his first chapter that they that are born again "are not born of blood [that is, the parents' blood] nor of the will of the flesh [not self-effort or goodness], nor of the will of man, but of God." God has no grandchildren.

God is truthful and man is sinful. One lesson remains from these verses: *Christ is merciful.* At the end of the list of the names comes the name of the Lord Jesus Christ. Though He is the Eternal God, He humbled Himself to become man, that He might provide salvation for sinners. What an amazing condescension! "For ye know the grace of our Lord Jesus Christ that though he was rich yet for your sakes he became poor that ye through his poverty might be rich" (II Cor. 8:9).

May we always read this list of names of Christ's lineage with thankful hearts. Here we observe that no one who partakes of human nature can be beyond the reach of the divine nature — beyond the reach of Christ's sympathy and compassion. If Jesus was not ashamed to be born of a woman whose lineage contained such names as those listed in this Scripture verse, then we need not think that He will be ashamed to call us brethren and to give us eternal life.

"As a Moabitess, taken into that line from whence the Messiah was to spring, and actually made an instrument of continuing the succession whereby he was brought into the world, Ruth was a witness for God to the Gentile world that He had not utterly forsaken them; but that they in due time should be incorporated with his chosen people, and become partakers of his salvation. Previous to this period, she was barren; but now she bore a son, through whom thousands and myriads were born to God: and in being the lineal ancestor of Christ, she was instrumental to the happiness of all that shall be saved by Him, even of us Gentiles, as well as of those that were of Jewish descent. Let none then apprehend that they are so far off, but that they may yet be brought nigh by the blood of Jesus, and 'sit down with Abraham, Isaac, and Jacob, in the kingdom of God.' "[5]

An elderly unattractive lady who after a life of wickedness and unbelief had been converted, became the object of persecution at the hands of her godless neighbors. They sought to anger her

---

[5] Charles Simeon, *Expository Outlines,* Vol. 3, pp. 107, 108.

and to disturb and upset the spirit of patience and lovingkindness that possessed her following her conversion to Christ. Finally, one of her persecutors, after having exhausted all of her resources, venomously exclaimed to her, "I think that you are the ugliest old woman that I have ever seen." To which the dear lady replied, with the tears freely flowing down her cheeks, "Isn't it wonderful that Christ can love an ugly old woman like me?" I ask you, "Isn't it wonderful that He can love sinners such as you and I?"

> Let not conscience make you linger,
> Nor of fitness fondly dream;
> All the fitness He requireth,
> Is to feel your need of Him.

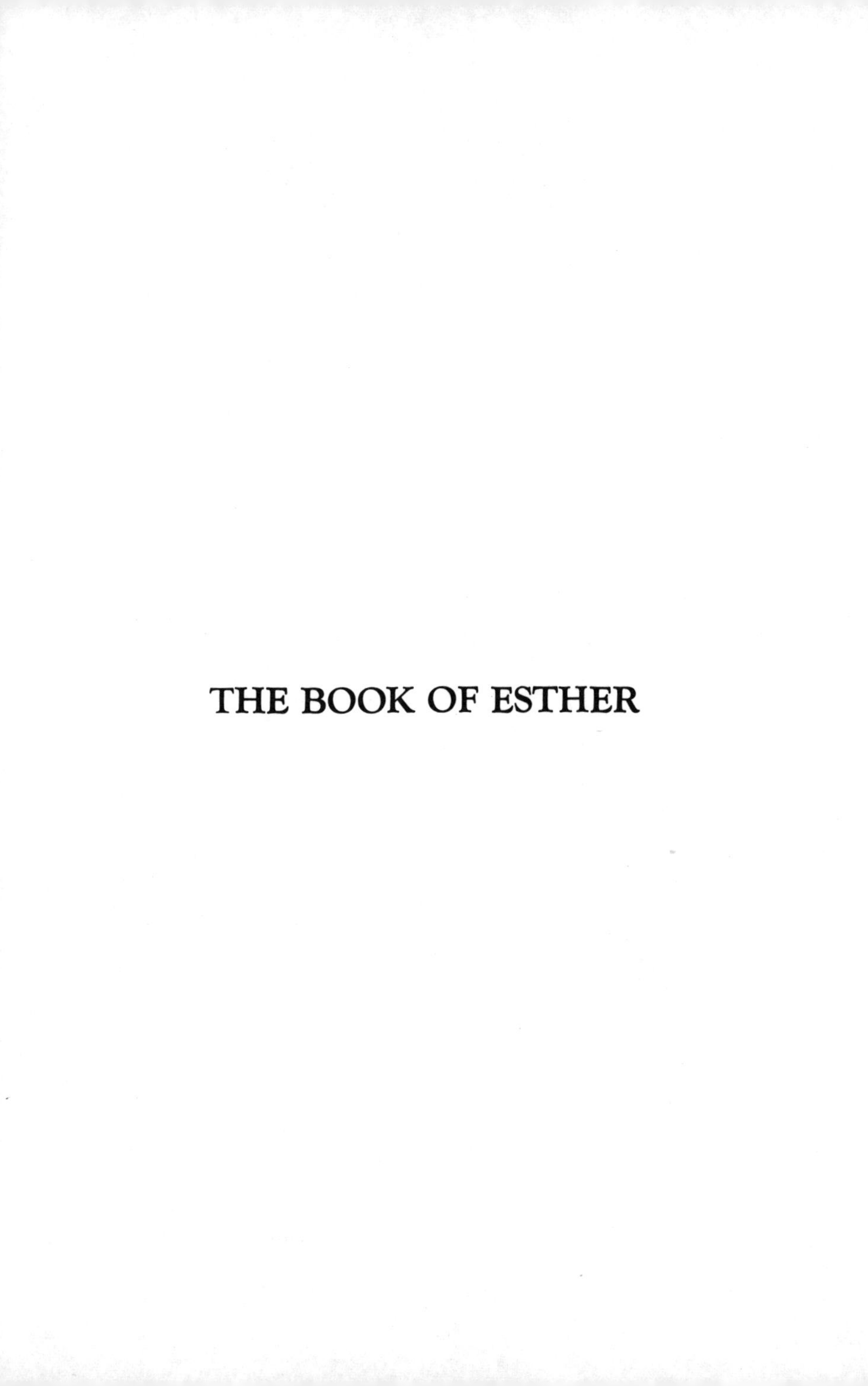

THE BOOK OF ESTHER

THE INTRODUCTION TO THE BOOK OF ESTHER —

AN INSPECTION

I. THE SETTING

The action of the story told in the book of Esther took place in Susa, the capital city of the nation of Persia. The book begins with an account of the king Ahasuerus sitting "on the throne of his kingdom, which was in Shushan, the palace" (1:2).

G. Campbell Morgan has suggested that "the events recorded in the book of Esther occurred between the completion of the Temple and the mission of Ezra (between Ezra 6 and 7). In all likelihood the narrative, as we have it, was taken directly from the Persian records."[1] The King of Persia, here called Ahasuerus, was Xerxes, whose reign was from 486-465 B.C. The events recorded in the book took place when the Jews were captives in Persia.

The Oriental court was one of great splendor and ostentation. It was not unusual for a Persian king to entertain several thousand at a banquet. Records indicate that the great pillared halls in the beautiful palaces could accommodate many hundreds, if not thousands of guests. The palace was elaborately and lavishly decorated.

Not all of the action took place in the palace, of course. Some of it was in other parts of the city and in the surrounding country and provinces. At the same time that the king was entertaining the nobles in the palace, the queen Vashti made a feast for the women in the royal house belonging to the king.

II. THE SYNOPSIS

King Ahasuerus (Xerxes) ruled a vast territory which extended all the way from India to Ethiopia, comprising in all one hundred twenty-seven provinces. In the third year of his rule he made a great feast for the powerful nobles, princes, and servants who ruled under him in the various provinces. His purpose

---

[1] *An Exposition of the Whole Bible.* Copyright 1959 by Fleming H. Revell Company. All rights reserved, p. 197.

was to "show the riches of his glorious kingdom and the honor of his excellent majesty" (1:4). The convocation lasted for a half of a year (180 days, verse 4). At the end of the one hundred eighty days the king prepared a great feast for all of his guests.

The description of the feast indicated that it was no ordinary gathering, but was characterized by all of the ostentation and display common to an Oriental court of that day. On the seventh day of the revelry, "when the heart of the king was merry with wine" (1:10), he asked to have Vashti the queen brought to the banquet hall so that he could exhibit her rare beauty before all the nobles.

Queen Vashti refused to appear at the summons of the king. This rebuff caused the king to become extremely angry. He had thought to display his absolute authority and was now to become a laughing stock to his people. His advisors suggested to him that the queen's contempt for the king would have a debilitating effect upon all of the nobles, for with the example of the queen, their wives would also resist authority. Hence, upon the recommendation of his counsellors, Ahasuerus had Vashti deposed as the queen. The fact that her refusal to appear before the king was publicly known made it mandatory that she be publicly disgraced. Women of the day were often only the pawns and playthings of men.

In the second chapter of the book there is recorded the appearance of Mordecai and Esther. Apparently Mordecai had brought up Esther, his cousin, almost as a daughter. While the king was seeking to find a new queen, Esther's beauty came to his attention. She was selected in competition with all of the other young virgins that were brought before the king. When this happened Mordecai advised Esther not to reveal her Jewish nationality to the king.

By refusing to bow before Haman, the chief minister to the king, Mordecai incurred his wrath and displeasure. Haman determined not only to do away with Mordecai, but also to exterminate all of his people, the Jews. By a clever maneuver, he secured the king's permission to proceed with his crafty plans. A delay of a year was given, no doubt so that thorough plans for complete extermination could be developed.

When Mordecai became informed of the planned massacre he called for fasting and prayer on the part of the Jews. He asked Esther the queen to intercede before the king. "Who knoweth whether thou art come to the kingdom for such a time as this?" (4:14).

Haman, anticipating the eventual fulfillment of his decree, had a gallows erected upon which he intended to take the life of Mordecai. In the meantime the king, unable to sleep one night, had some chronicles and records read to him. The account read to him reminded him of how on a previous occasion Mordecai had discovered a plot against the king's life and had been the instrument to save him. The king inquired as to what reward had been given to Mordecai for this gracious deed and was told that nothing had been done for him.

The king then called Haman and inquired of him as to what he thought should be done for the man whom the king wished to honor. The proud and crafty Haman, thinking that this man could be none other than himself, suggested that great public honor should be accorded this individual, that he should be attired in royal apparel, a crown placed upon his head, and that he should then ride on horseback through the street to the acclaim of the multitudes. To his utter dismay, Haman was then ordered by the king to confer this honor upon none other than Mordecai.

At the queen's banquet, which followed, she revealed to the king, Haman's diabolical plan for the destruction of all of the Jews: "For we are sold, I and my people, to be destroyed, to be slain, and to perish" (7:4). When the king perceived the treachery of the plot against the Jews he ordered Haman to be hanged upon the gallows which he had prepared for Mordecai. Since the royal decree for the execution of the Jews could not be recalled or rescinded, the king sent out another decree which would allow the Jews to defend themselves against any who would try to kill them. The Jews thus emerged victorious over their enemies and the Feast of Purim was instituted to celebrate and perpetuate the observance of this deliverance.

The book concludes with the account of Mordecai being elevated to the prime ministership and next to the king in authority. He was also honored among his own people and "accepted of the multitude of his brethren, seeking the wealth of his people, and speaking peace to all his seed" (10:3).

III. THE STYLE

The book is written in a dramatic and moving style with a great deal of exciting action taking place. In contrast to the book of Ruth which may be described as a "pastoral" or idyll,

the book of Esther is written in the form of an historical chroni-
cle or record. The book of Ruth portrays beautifully and ap-
pealingly the domestic and real life experiences of the individuals of a family, while the book of Esther has to do with how
God spared a whole nation. The book of Ruth tells the story
of humble folk and the rural life, while the book of Esther is
concerned with the experiences of kings, queens, and nobles
with the setting in a great Oriental city.

The book of Ruth details God's providence and care for His
people as individuals, while the book of Esther relates how the
God of history raises up and destroys nations.

It is most unusual that in the book there is no specific reference even to God's name. However His providential care for
His own chosen people is nowhere more evident than in this
story.

The language and style of the book of Esther is very similar
to that of the Chronicles, and of Ezra and Nehemiah which it
follows.

Chapter 1

VASHTI VANQUISHED (1:1-22)

The Persian Empire was one of the great empires of the ancient world. King Ahasuerus ruled a vast territory divided into 127 provinces extending from India to Ethiopia. He was an absolute monarch exercising unlimited authority over the life and death of his subjects. Secular history records something of the cruelty of his character. "The man who led two millions of soldiers against the Greeks, who scourged the sea, and put to death the engineers of his bridge because their work was injured by a storm, was the same man who insulted his queen for her modesty, and who was ready to massacre a people in order to gratify a favorite."[1]

In order to properly impress the princes and nobles of the provinces with his power and authority, he called them to the capital where for 180 days they were entertained. The "riches of his glorious kingdom and the honor of his excellent majesty" were displayed (1:4).

I. A ROYAL REPAST (1:1-9)

Following the 180 days of convocation given to instruction in the rule of government and state policy, King Ahasuerus made a great feast which was to continue for seven days. It is thought by some scholars that this great occasion preceded the preparation for the expedition into Greece which came to such disastrous an end.

Nothing was spared to make this great feast worthy of the splendor and majesty of the mighty monarch. The garden court surrounding the palace was in its height of beauty. The main dining hall was decorated with awnings of white, green, and blue fastened or supported by silver rings attached to the pillars of marble. The couches on which the guests reclined were of gold and silver. The flooring was made of variously colored stones or mosaics.

Wine from the king's own private stores flowed in abun-

---

[1] *The Book of Esther*, Pulpit Commentary, p. 4.

dance, served from golden goblets. The guests apparently partook of the lavish supply of food, fruit, and drink for seven days. It appears that the motive for all of the ostentation, gluttony and carousing was to flatter the vanity of the king. There is no evidence that the king was concerned to improve the lot and condition of his subjects, but rather that he was motivated to flatter his own ego and pamper his own vanity.

In contrast to the fleeting splendor of the king's great banquet, let us be reminded of the royal repast which the King of Kings has prepared for all of his royal subjects. They are invited to "come and dine." The table is spread. There is "feasting at Jesus' table all the time." In the wonderful "gospel feast" there is no ostenation or display, but a genuine manifestation of God's love and provision for all of His children.

A story was told by Rowland Hill of a hard working man in England years ago who fell on evil days. Through no fault of his own he lost health, situation, and all of his capital. Together with his family he was face to face with ruin. A rich man heard of his need, and sent the distressed man a note for twenty-five dollars in an envelope with these words attached, "More to follow." After a few days, the rich friend sent another note of the same amount with the same phrase, "More to follow." For many weeks the broken family received a constant stream of bank notes always with the same cheering message, "More to follow," until their ruined fortune was mended, and a measure of their prosperity restored.

So it is with God's gifts. He gives enough for present needs and there is always the cheering assurance, "More to follow."

II. A REGRETTABLE REQUEST (1:10, 11)

Both the sacred records and secular history indicate that King Ahasurerus displayed a great deal of pride, self-indulgence, extravagance, and vain-glory. On the seventh day of the celebration when "the heart of the king was merry with wine" (1:10), he sent a message by his chamberlains to Vashti, his queen. He desired her to make an appearance at the banquet for the nobles that he might exhibit her beauty, "for she was fair to look on" (1:11).

It is apparent that the king was not only intoxicated with pride, but also with wine.

Intoxication destroys sane judgment. King Ahasuerus had already devoted 180 days showing to the nobles practically all that he possessed. Now his foggy mind suggests one more thing of beauty to display to the gaze of the men. His intention no doubt was to present the queen un-veiled before all of the assembled guests. This was in complete disregard of the proper observance of Persian decorum and etiquette. In his right mind he would never have thought of committing such an outrage.

Intoxication occasions shame. To have obeyed the king would have brought open shame to the queen. And when the queen refused the disgraceful request it brought feelings of shame and anger to the king himself. How could he rule a nation when he could not control his own queen? All of the people would know of the refusal of the queen to obey the king's command..

Intoxication brings regret. When the king would be sober again, he would regret his folly. He had lowered himself in the sight, not only of his queen, but of his subjects throughout the entire kingdom. We read in the first verse of Chapter 2 that the king "remembered Vashti, and what she had done, and what was decreed against her" (2:1).

Evangeline Booth of the Salvation Army said, "Drink has shed more blood, hung more crepe, sold more homes, plunged more people into bankruptcy, armed more villains, slain more children, snapped more wedding rings, defiled more innocence, blinded more eyes, dethroned more reason, wrecked more manhood, dishonored more womanhood, broken more hearts, blasted more lives, driven more to suicide and dug more graves than any other scourge that has cursed the world."

"I am the greatest criminal in history. I have killed more men than have fallen in all the wars of the world. I have turned men into brutes. I have made millions of homes unhappy. I have transformed many ambitious youths into hopeless parasites. I make smooth the downward path for countless millions. I destroy the weak and weaken the strong. I make the wise man a fool and trample the fool in his folly. I ensnare the innocent. The abandoned wife knows me; the hungry children know me. I have ruined millions and shall try to ruin more. Do you know me? I am alcohol" (H. W. Gibson).

III. A REGAL REFUSAL (1:12)

Queen Vashti refused to obey the king's command to appear before him and his nobles. She sent back a message by the chamberlains that she did not intend to appear. She no doubt knew that her refusal could result not only in her removal, but also in her death.

History does not give us any further information about Vashti, except to say that she was the queen. She "made a feast for the women in the royal house which belonged to King Ahasuerus" (1:9). She was not only "fair to look on" (1:11), but she was of queenly and noble bearing.

Her refusal to honor the king's command was a costly sacrifice. She must have known that grave consequences would follow her refusal to obey the king. Actually, it might be argued that the king had commanded what was really unlawful, at least a serious violation of custom. The women of that day were kept in seclusion and were veiled. They were not even allowed to expose their countenances to the gaze of strangers. Now for a modest woman to be ordered to display her charms before a large company of drunken revellers was unthinkable. It is true that women of that day were considered more as chattels than as individuals, and as such were under the absolute authority of their husbands. But when the husband required what was morally wrong, an honorable woman had no choice but to refuse. The queen was deposed simply for daring to protect her womanly honor.

Queen Vashti was an example of one who chose to take a stand for what was right in the face of whatever consequences might follow. She was true to herself and a credit and an example to all women.

We may also observe that Queen Vashti's refusal might be looked upon as an illustration of Divine providence. Vashti's removal from her position opened the way for the deliverance of the Jews through Queen Esther from the certain destruction which would be planned for them. To follow the right course of action, regardless of the cost, brings eternal dividends.

"Two men were once discussing why it is that you cannot see the stars by day. The stars are still there; the distance is not greater by day than by night; why, then, cannot these mighty lamps be seen by day? One man maintained that they could be seen if one went far enough down in a well. The other denied the proposition but permitted himself to be lowered into the well. After he had been lowered a certain distance, he was asked if he could see the stars, and said, 'No.' Still farther down the same question was asked, with the same answer. But when he had been lowered to a great depth, then, looking up toward the heavens, he said he was able to see the stars. Go down deep enough into a well, and you can see the stars by day. So to those who are willing to co-operate with God, and to will for themselves the things which he hath willed for them, the deep well of adversity and trouble is a place whence they can see the stars of the spiritual heavens and know that in all and above all and through all is God, and that God is love."[2]

We know nothing more about what happened to Queen Vashti, but in the adversity which came to her, she need have no regrets but that she had done what was right and proper for one in her position to do. "The one redeeming feature in the revelation of conditions at the court of Ahasuerus was Vashti's refusal to obey the king. She paid the price of her loyalty to her womanhood in being deposed."[3]

IV. A RUINOUS REVENGE (1:13-22)

It would seem that the punishment inflicted upon Queen Vashti was completely out of proportion to her misdemeanor, if such it might be considered. The cruel and despotic king whose word was law, in his anger turned to his counsellors for their advice as to what should be done to the queen. Their suggestion was that Queen Vashti should be deposed for refusing to honor the King's command. "If it please the king, let there go a royal commandment from him, and let it be written among the laws of the Persians and the Medes, that it be not altered, That Vashti come no more before king Ahasuerus; and let the king give her royal estate unto another that is better than she" (1:19).

The Queen's refusal, as interpreted by the counsellors, would give encouragement to all wives in the entire realm to disobey their husbands. "For this deed of the queen shall come abroad unto all women, so that they shall despise their husbands in their eyes, when it shall be reported, The king Ahasuerus commanded Vashti the queen to be brought in before him, but she came not" (1:17).

It should be pointed out that in relation to the divine order of the sexes, in which the husband is to be the head of the wife, Queen Vashti had displayed disobedience and even defiance of the King's command. However, as has been observed, the command was unreasonable and untenable. For the queen to have complied would have been to commit an outrage against her own modesty and purity.

Though it was cruel and inhuman to dethrone the queen for refusing to obey the unreasonable demand of an intoxicated husband, there was no recourse open to her but to acquiesce to

---

2 *Macartney's Illustrations*, p. 397.

3 G. Campbell Morgan, *The Analyzed Bible*, p. 150.

the king's command. History records little else concerning Queen Vashti, but her name. But her uncompromising stand in the face of apparent ruin and defeat, mark her as a real queen.

"The name of Vashti appears to view for only a moment; it then utterly disappears — and in disgrace. Yet not in shame; neither in the shame of sin or folly, nor in the shame even of error of judgment and want of true wisdom."[4]

The counsellors encouraged the king to send letters to all of his subjects making a decree that "every man should bear rule in his own house" (1:22). This was a proper order, but the queen's resolve should not be taken as the reason for it. Had the queen been involved in some wrong-doing this might have affected all women adversely, but her conduct could not be given this kind of interpretation. Rather, her uncompromising stand against that which she knew would be wrong for her would have a strengthening affect upon all others of her sex if they should be placed in similar compromising situations.

Nonetheless the queen's fate was sealed because of the king's pride and passion and because his word was law.

---

[4] *The Book of Esther*, Pulpit Commentary, p. 24.

Chapter 2

ESTHER ENTHRONED (2:1-23)

"After these things," so begins Chapter 2 of the book of Esther. It is thought that there was a two year period of time between the great assembly that Ahasuerus (Xerxes) held at the palace (483 B.C.) and his departure for Greece (481 B.C.) and that during this time the events of Chapter 2 took place.

I. AN UNAVAILING CONCERN (2:1)

"When the wrath of King Ahasuerus was appeased, he remembered Vashti, and what she had done, and what was decreed against her" (2:1). Memory cannot lightly be dismissed. It stores up events and attitudes that later on may return with haunting force. "Ahasuerus remembered Vashti." We may read between the lines here something of the regret of the king at his remembered reaction to Vashti's refusal to comply with his request.

The poet Shakespeare had Mark Antony utter over the body of Julius Caesar the words: "The evil that men do lives after them; The good is oft interred with their bones." In this instance through God's overruling providence the evil deed of Ahasuerus against Vashti would still perform His will. It was however now too late for the king to alter his decision, and whatever his regret might have been, he could not undo his deed. We may find both profit and warning in what memory brings back of that which was either unpleasant or unworthy, as well as that which was pleasant or worthy.

II. AN UNRESTRAINED CONDUCT (2:2-4)

In order to placate the king the advisors who had counselled Vashti's disgrace now suggested to him an equally disgraceful plan. The plan was to seek out all of the "fair young virgins" from all parts of the realm. They were to be brought to the palace, and after the prescribed "beauty treatments," they were to appear one by one before the king. The one who most pleased the king would then become queen in place of Vashti.

"And the thing pleased the king" (2:4). "The novelty of it

arrested him; the pleasure which it promised charmed him; all memories and regrets were speedily swallowed up in the anticipated delights of a new self-indulgence."[1] The conduct here described, while not to be sanctioned or condoned in a Christian culture or society, was nonetheless used by God to bring about His own purposes in behalf of His chosen people.

III. AN UNQUESTIONING CONFIDENCE (2:5-14)

We are now introduced to Mordecai, a Jew, "who had been carried away from Jerusalem with the captives who had been carried away with Jeconiah [Jehoiachin], King of Judah, whom Nebuchadnezzar, the king of Baylon, had carried away" (2:6).

Mordecai had raised a young Jewess, Esther by name, as his own daughter following the deaths of her own father and mother. She was actually his uncle's daughter. We may be quite certain that as a godly Jew he had instructed Esther in the worship of God and in the ways of the Jewish people. This is evident in what subsequently took place. Mordecai had confidence in Esther's understanding of her own destiny.

It is apparent also that Esther had an unquestioning confidence in the will of God for her own life. There is no indication given that she sought for any recognition, but that she together with all of the other maidens became unwittingly involved in the King's plan in the choice of his new queen. Esther is described as "fair and beautiful" (2:7). This was not only a beauty of face and form, but of character and integrity also.

When she was brought before Hegai, the king's chamberlain, keeper of the women, she immediately "pleased him and obtained kindness from him" (2:9). She and the women assigned to her were moved to the "best place of the house of the women." Esther did not reveal her people nor her nationality as Mordecai had directed. He kept in touch with her every day, "to know how she did, and what should become of her" (2:11).

Each of the maidens was given a year's time of preparation and beautification before being brought before the king. The plan was that if any maiden especially pleased him, he would request her return. Otherwise she was returned to the "second house of the women," after spending a night with the king.

IV. AN UNAFFECTED COMPOSURE (2:15, 16)

When Esther's turn came to be presented to the king, "she

---

[1] *The Book of Esther*, Pulpit Commentary, p. 51.

required nothing but what Hegai, the king's chamberlain, the keeper of the women, appointed." She did not ask for any special favors nor did she require them. In spite of this the record states that "Esther obtained favor in the sight of all them who looked upon her" (2:15). She had natural grace and beauty which went far deeper than merely the physical.

V. AN UNEXPECTED CORONATION (2:17-20)

It is recorded that "the king loved Esther above all the women, and she obtained grace and favor in his sight more than all the virgins, so that he set the royal crown upon her head and made her queen instead of Vashti" (2:17).

To be made the queen was not an honor that Esther had sought. Her exaltation is another of the numerous instances in the Scripture of how God raised up the unlikely to be crowned with honor and glory. Joseph sold into bondage became the prime minister of Egypt. David the shepherd boy became the king of Israel. Here illustrated, Esther an orphan girl became the queen of all Persia.

Esther's coronation as the queen was celebrated at a great feast, called Esther's feast. The king cancelled certain taxes and gave gifts to signal his pleasure. As has already been noted, Esther's exaltation was to bring an unexcelled opportunity to fulfill the purpose of God for His chosen people. She would not forget Mordecai's instruction and counsel given her while she was cared for by him. She did not at this point reveal her kindred nor her race. She kept the trust of Mordecai. She retained the sweet grace of humility and sought only to do the will of God.

VI. AN UNSOLICITED CONFRONTATION (2:21-23)

The final verses of Chapter 2 tell how Mordecai, the Jew, was instrumental in saving the king's life. Two of the king's chamberlains, Bigthan and Teresh, of those "who kept the door," guarded the entrance to the king's sleeping quarters, became angry for some unstated reason and sought to lay hands on the king.

Mordecai discovered the plot and gave the information to Esther who communicated it to the king. An investigation was conducted, and the plotters were discovered and summarily hanged for their treason against the king. The record of the attempted assassination was placed in the "book of the chronicles before the king" (2:23). Apparently the king did not give im-

mediate attention to rewarding Mordecai for his discovery of
the plot. In Chapter 6 the account of the attempted assassination
comes to the king's attention and results in high honor being
accorded Mordecai.

Chapter 3

HAMAN'S HATRED (3:1-15)

An unknown interval of time, perhaps even a few years, may well have occurred between Chapters 2 and 3 of the book. We are introduced to a man named Haman, the son of Hammedatha, the Agagite, whom King Ahasuerus promoted to be the second in the kingdom in authority and prestige (3:1). A special command was given by the king that all should bow before Haman in reverence and respect. Only one man, Mordecai the Jew, refused to do homage to Haman.

I. HAMAN'S PRIDE (3:1, 2)

It is not difficult to understand how the favor of the king caused Haman to be lifted up in his own esteem. Along with the king's approval was the homage paid him by the others in the king's court. But this sudden and perhaps unexpected acclaim was to prove a great danger to Haman, though no doubt he did not realize this. He had apparently quickly risen to power and prominence, but he was not to be able to long enjoy what was now his by right of his elevation. A test would soon be made that would immediately reveal Haman's pride and haughty spirit. The truth expressed in Proverbs 16:18 is a timeless one: "Pride goeth before destruction, and an haughty spirit before a fall."

II. MORDECAI'S PRACTICE (3:2-4)

"Mordecai bowed not, nor did obeisance to Haman" (3:2). What was behind his refusal to comply with the prevailing custom of the court? Did he not know better? Was he not afraid that he would be called to give account of his behavior? His seeming lack of respect was noted by the other servants of the court, and they finally asked him, "Why transgresseth thou the king's commandment?" (3:3).

Did he refuse to bow because he was disloyal to the king? This could not be the case for he had recently saved the king's life by reporting the plot against the king's life. Did he have a personal antipathy to the king's favorite? Probably not, at least not at this point.

There was one compelling reason for his refusal to bow. He gave worship to One only — the God of Abraham, Isaac, and Jacob. Ah, he was a Jew who believed in the commandment to worship God alone! And so he must take his stand, even though it meant standing alone. His practice was to bow only before his Sovereign, his God. His purpose was to maintain a proper conduct and witness a good confession. When he realized that his silence was not understood, he then declared his Jewish origin and faith.

Here is a powerful and timely example for our day. We must not be afraid to declare our faith in God nor be ashamed to witness for Christ even if it means standing alone. We do well to recall the words of Martin Luther when he stood before Charles V to answer the charge of heresy. He boldly declared, "Here I stand; I cannot do otherwise; God help me. Amen."

A group of young college men had one evening made a trip from Princeton to New York City. When they arrived in the city they agreed that they would go together to a certain place, a place where soul and body could well be defiled. That is, they all agreed, but one. He had the courage of his faith and conviction to say no. Later, he looked back upon that refusal as the turning point of his life, and the point from which he was led into a life of service for his Lord.

III. HAMAN'S PREJUDICE (3:5-7)

When Haman saw that Mordecai "bowed not nor did him reverence," he was filled with almost uncontrollable anger. He determined upon taking revenge not only upon Mordecai, but upon all of his people, the Jews. Here we note a prejudice and proposed revenge that was far out of proportion to the imagined "crime" committed by Mordecai. "A trivial slight was so laid to heart that it aroused a ferocious spirit, for the satisfaction of which no shedding of blood, no desolation of cities, could suffice."[1] "Wherefore Haman sought to destroy all the Jews that were throughout the whole kingdom of Ahasuerus, even the people of Mordecai" (3:6).

Following his decision to annihilate the Jews, Haman determined to select the proper and appropriate time for the slaughter by casting lots, a practice which was prevalent in Eastern cultures when any act of consequence or significance was to be carried out. This superstitious practice employed the

---

[1] *The Book of Esther*, Pulpit Commentary, p. 64.

use of dice, the use of pieces of wood, or even slips of parchment. The Jews too believed that in the casting of lots God would give direction. This is the meaning of Proverbs 16:33: "The lot is cast into the lap, but the whole disposing thereof is of the Lord."

By chance the date was then determined. It was to be the thirteenth day of the twelfth month of Adar which was some ten months distant. No doubt Haman would have preferred an earlier date, but he dared not break with the date selected by Pur, "that is, the lot" (3:7).

IV. AHASUERUS' PERMISSION (3:8-15)

The date being now determined, Haman went to king Ahasuerus to secure his permission to carry out his villianous plan. He was most desirous to secure the king's approval, and so he suggested to him that the Jews had certain peculiar laws which were not in keeping with the laws of the realm, and which prevented them from obeying the Persian laws in toto. This naturally prejudiced the king against the Jews, and so he gave ready acquiescence to the plan for their destruction.

To further make certain of the king's approval, Haman offered to pay into the royal treasuries when the assignment was completed the sum of ten thousand talents of silver (3:9). (One talent of silver would today be worth about $1940. 10,000 x $1940 equals $19,400,000.[2] The king readily accepted the offer of this handsome "bribe," took his ring from his hand and gave it to Haman thus sealing the transaction and giving his consent "to do with them (the Jews) as it seemeth good to thee." Not only were the Jews given into Haman's hand, but their silver also (3:11).

The king's scribes were called, the order for the extermination of the Jews was written and sealed with the king's ring, and the letters were sent by post to all of the provinces with authority "to destroy, to kill, and to cause to perish, all Jews, both young and old, little children and women, in one day, even upon the thirteenth day of the twelfth month, which is the month Adar, and to take the property of them for spoil" (3:13).

The carriers of the letters went out with the news, and the decree was also published in Shushan, the palace. "And the

---

[2] See note in *New Scofield Reference Bible* at Exodus 30:13.

king and Haman sat down to drink; but the city Shushan was perplexed" (3:15).

What a contrast is to be found in these two statements! "The king and Haman sat down to drink, but the city was perplexed." Here is described heartless indifference to the possibility of human suffering. Here is the picture of the depravity of mankind even though civilization may apply a coating of thin veneer over man's bestiality. Nero fiddled while Rome burned, and Herod feasted when he had John the Baptist cast into prison. It is also more than probable that they drank to still the voices of their own consciences.

In his book *Toilers of the Sea* Victor Hugo says: "You can no more keep thought from returning to past transgression than keep the sea from returning to the shore after it has gone out. In the sea we call it the tide; but the guilty man calls it conscience. Conscience heaves the soul as the tide does the ocean."

Haman would live to regret his diabolical plan, and die the death himself for its evil conception.

Chapter 4

TIMELY TESTIMONY (4:1-17)

It is quite certain that Haman waited to make public his secret intention to have the Jews exterminated until he had secured the king's permission and until the complete plans for the slaughter had been approved. But as soon as he was confident that the whole scheme had proceeded beyond the king's power to recall, the evil tidings were published abroad.

I. INFORMATION IMPARTED (4:1-7)

The news finally broke! It was the "talk of the town." Every city, town, hamlet, and village throughout the vast Persian Empire received the word. "When Mordecai perceived all that was done, he tore his clothes, and put on sackcloth with ashes, and went out into the center of the city, and cried with a loud and a bitter cry" (4:1). The sad news of destruction was overwhelming. The use of either sackcloth or of ashes by themselves would have indicated deep grief. The use of both of them together indicated the deepest possible agony of spirit and despair. It was not alone for himself that Mordecai was concerned, but for his people.

Mordecai gave the first note of lamentation, and as the news reached around the realm, the cry was taken up by the Jews throughout the entire empire. "And in every province, wherever the king's commandment and his decree came, there was great mourning among the Jews, and fasting, and weeping, and wailing; and many lay in sackcloth and ashes" (4:3).

The news of Mordecai's strange behavior before the king's gate was finally communicated to Queen Esther in the palace by her maids and chamberlains. Esther was "exceedingly grieved, and sent raiment to clothe Mordecai, and to take away his sackcloth from him, but he received it not" (4:4).

Apparently Esther did not yet know of the awful plot to do away with her people. This is evident in her sending Hathach, who attended her, to Mordecai to find out what was the cause of his grief (4:5).

Mordecai told the whole sordid story to Hathach including a

reference to the "exact sum of money that Haman had promised to pay to the king's treasuries for the Jews, to destroy them" (4:7). He also sent with Hathach a copy of the writing of the decree to show to Esther and to explain it to her.

II. INTERVENTION IMPLORED (4:8-14)

With the explanation given to Esther by Hathach, Mordecai also charged Esther that "she should go in unto the king, to make supplication unto him, and to make request before him for her people" (4:8).

Upon receiving this urgent request from Mordecai that she should intervene before the king, Esther sent word back to him that if any one came before the king without an invitation to do so, he or she could be put to death. "This was a reasonable law in such a country. It gave protection to the king against attempts at assassination. But like most sensible laws or restrictions it affected the loyal as well as the disloyal. The queen was bound by the same law as the would-be criminal."[1] Only if the king would hold forth the "golden scepter" to such an one could he live. And then Esther added the very serious word to Mordecai, "I have not been called to come in unto the king these thirty days" (4:11).

It must be remembered that the Persian king was an absolute monarch. He had the power of life and death in his hands. Queen Esther would have to come into his presence at the peril of her own life. The golden scepter would be extended when the king pleased as an indication that he would grant a hearing.

What a great blessing it is to know that the Eternal Almighty King with whom we have to do always holds forth the "golden scepter" of welcome, of mercy, and of pardon. We are invited to come boldly into His presence whenever we so desire. We may have an audience with Him at any time.

Said Phillips Brooks of prayer: "Prayer is not the overcoming of God's reluctance; it is the taking hold of God's willingness."

We may be certain that God will hear the faintest cry of one of His children. A life-guard at a great city bathing beach was once asked how he could possibly hear and know when someone was in need of rescue when there were hundreds of bathers on the beach and in the water making such a hub-bub of noise. His reply was, "No matter how great the confusion and tumult

---

[1] Eric W. Hayden, Preaching through the Bible, Vol. 2, p. 87.

of noise there has never been a single time when I could not distinguish the cry of distress above it all. I can always tell it." How like God this is! In the midst of the noise and confusion of the world, God never fails to hear even the faintest cry of the soul that calls to Him for help amid the breakers and storms of life.

Mordecai was undaunted by Esther's message. He immediately sent back a most serious and challenging word to her, "Think not with thyself that thou shalt escape in the king's house, more than all the Jews" (4:13). Mordecai wanted to make crystal clear to Esther that even though she was in the palace she would be as vulnerable as the rest of the Jews, and that she would not escape because of her position. He added, "For if thou altogether holdest thy peace at this time, then shall there relief and deliverance arise to the Jews from another place, but thou and thy father's house shall be destroyed." He concluded his message to her with the striking statement, "And who knoweth whether thou art come to the kingdom for such a time as this?" (4:14).

"For such a time as this!" These words bring a thrill of contemplation and anticipation. Mordecai had faith to believe that somehow and from somewhere deliverance would come. But he placed squarely on her shoulders the grave responsibility that was hers. She was the answer to the Jews' salvation!

"We can imagine Esther saying to herself, 'Away with all my cowardice, my weak-heartedness. Why should I fear to go and plead for my people?' 'Can I be so unworthy of my descent as an Israelite? Will God forsake me when striving to save and serve his chosen people? Come, O thou that leddest thy people as a flock, and lead me now to a prosperous ending of my hazardous work! O thou that didst break the power of Pharaoh, restrain that of our enemy! O thou that didst go forth with Joshua and help him by hailstorms from heaven against the Amalekites, unsheathe thy sword against this Agagite, this Haman who seeks our hurt! Cause me, O God, like Miriam, to praise thee in gladsome song because the enemy and his designs are alike overthrown. Unworthy am I to be an instrument in thine hands; yet, if I come to the kingdom for such a time as this, make me ready to do thy will.' "[2]

We may learn from this beautiful example of courage and dedication on the part of Esther that we are all given oppor-

---

[2] *The Book of Esther,* Pulpit Commentary, p. 92.

tunities to do good, that these opportunities should not be missed, and that often the opportunity does not last long. We must "buy up" the time because the days are evil.

Clarance Macartney told the story of an old Saxon king who set out with his army to seek to put down a rebellion in a distant province of his kingdom. He was successful in quelling the insurrection and defeating the army of the rebels. Then, wanting to restore again these men to their former useful state in his realm, he placed a lighted candle over the archway of the castle at his headquarters, directing that all of the rebels who would surrender and pledge again their loyalty while the candle burned would be spared. He offered them the opportunity to secure mercy and pardon, but the offer was limited to the life of the candle.[3]

All great offers of life and of service have their "candle limitations." There is a limited period of time in which to make use of the offer and the opportunity. Tomorrow may be too late. "For such a time as this!"

III. INTERCESSION INTREATED (4:15-17)

Esther was willing to risk her life to save her people, but she realized that she needed the help of others in fasting, prayer, and intercession. She realized, as perhaps no one else could have, how serious was her assignment. She had not only to secure an audience with the king unbidden, thus risking her own life, but then she had to reveal to the king her own nationality which of itself would be the occasion for death by Haman's decree sanctioned by the king.

"Go, gather together all the Jews who are present in Shushan, and fast ye for me . . ." (4:16). Esther in this intreaty clearly revealed that her faith and confidence were in God and not in any man. She felt that she was "standing in the need of prayer," and sought help. She not only requested help from others, but was ready with her maidens to "fast likewise." This is most significant in that it speaks of the piety and witness of Esther before her own maidens who were a part of the pagan Oriental court, but who were now ready to pray to Esther's God. It is true that no specific mention is made of prayers, but the fast was all a prayer.

"And if I perish, I perish" (4:16). It was no feeble emotion that gripped the queen in her utterance of these courageous

---

[3] *Macartney's Illustrations,* p. 254.

words. Mordecai's request, her own identity with her people, and her love of life not only for herself but for all of the Jews, prompted her to be willing to risk her life. She knew that she was facing dire consequences, and prepared herself for the worst. "If I perish, I perish!" She counted not her own life too dear to sacrifice it for others. Her words were not the result of desperation, but were the words of godly heroism.

We cannot meditate upon these words of Esther's without being reminded of the words of our Lord while He prayed in the Garden prior to His crucifixion. He addressed His Father and said, "Nevertheless, not my will, but Thine be done." He was willing to die for the salvation of the world. Esther in her resolve and decision was a type of Israel's Messiah, ready to die for God's people.

Let us be reminded again that the way into the presence of our King, the King of Kings and Lord of Lords is open to all. He is near to all who will call upon Him. No one is refused a hearing. All are welcome to come through Christ, the Way, the Truth, and the Life.

Chapter 5

ESTHER'S ENTREATY (5:1-14)

As someone has pointed out, the first verse of this chapter is "full of royalty." Esther clothed herself in her *royal apparel* and appeared before the king who sat upon his *royal throne* in the *royal house.* It should be noted also that it was on "the third day," indicating that Esther had kept the agreed upon three-day fast.

We who once were members of the *"rebel family,"* but are now a part of God's *"royal family"* are welcome to come into the King's presence. We may draw near with boldness, but also with reverence. We may come with confidence remembering that "He that cometh to God must believe that he is, and that he is a rewarder of them that diligently seek him." We do not honor God when we come fearfully or distrustfully.

I. ESTHER'S COURAGE (5:1)

We are reminded from the previous chapter that anyone who approached the king unbidden might be put to death unless the king held out to him the golden scepter. There does not seem to be any indication of fear upon the part of the queen as she approached the royal throne although inwardly she might have trembled. And well she might, for the future destiny of Israel rested upon her frail shoulders at this point in her career as queen. This was no assignment for a coward.

The king was no doubt suprised, but evidently pleased as his eyes, turned toward the door, saw the graceful and beautiful form of his young queen dressed in her royal apparel waiting to be recognized. "She obtained favor in his sight" (5:2).

II. AHASUERUS' COMPLIMENT (5:2-8)

The king immediately held out the golden scepter toward Esther. The scepter was probably a rod overlaid with gold to which was attached at the tip a golden ball. "Esther drew near and touched the top of the scepter" (5:2). This was an indication of her humility and no doubt caused the affection of the king's heart to be revived toward her.

"Then said the king to her, What wilt thou Queen Esther? And what is thy request? It shall be even given thee to the half of the kingdom" (5:3). The offer of "half of the kingdom" should probably not be given an actual literal interpretation. This appeared to be an Oriental saying which rather meant the extension of a special favor. Esther must have understood it to mean that she would have a gracious hearing from the king.

"And Esther answered, If it seem good unto the king, let the king and Haman come this day unto the banquet that I have prepared for him. Then the king said, Cause Haman to make haste, that he may do as Esther hath said. So the king and Haman came to the banquet that Esther had prepared." (5:4, 5).

We may well wonder why Esther did not at once present her petition to the king. Perhaps it was her sense of God's leading, and maybe even her womanly intuition and instinct that caused her to delay and to defer her request. She made use of the technique of suspense also which no doubt made the king even more curious to know what she wanted. Perhaps on the other hand, she desired more time so that her courage might be strengthened.

At any rate at the banquet when the king asked her the second time what her petition was, and suggested again that he would grant it even to the half of his kingdom (5:6), Esther simply invited him and Haman to come to a second banquet on the next day (5:7, 8). Then, she indicated, she would answer his question and state her wish. It appeared that the overruling providence of God was at work occasioning the delay and the banquet appointment for the next day. The delay would certainly give more time for Haman's true spirit of wickedness and heartlessness to be revealed and observed.

Haman went home "joyful and with a glad heart" (5:9). Just to think that he was to dine a second time at a royal banquet the next day in the presence of the king and queen!

III. MORDECAI'S CONTEMPT (5:9)

Passing the king's gate on the way to his home, Haman saw Mordecai, the Jew, and observed again that he neither stood to reverence him, nor moved aside, nor trembled for him. Previously Mordecai would not bow nor prostrate himself before Haman, and now he did not even acknowledge his presence. This open contempt on the part of Mordecai for the person and presence of Haman was particularly galling and irritating to Haman.

IV. HAMAN'S CONSTERNATION (5:10-13)

Haman restrained his anger for the moment though we may be certain that Mordecai's attitude greatly irritated him. Haman went home, called his wife Zeresh and his close friends together, and proceeded to give them the account of his many successes and his glorious accomplishments. He enumerated all of the things that the king had done for him including his promotion and advancement above all of the other princes and servants of the king's realm (5:10, 11).

He also related how Esther the queen had chosen him alone to be at the banquet with the king and queen on the following day. All of this had "gone to his head."

But then he made the unhappy admission: "Yet all this availeth me nothing, as long as I see Mordecai, the Jew, sitting at the king's gate" (5:13). The "fly in the ointment" was Mordecai. Haman had had a phenomenal rise to fame and fortune. He had become second only to the king in the entire realm in prestige and power. How proud he was! Though he did not realize it, he was in a very dangerous position. His happiness and satisfaction were marred by the attitude of one lowly Jew. "Pride goeth before destruction and a haughty spirit before a fall."

When a man boasted in the presence of Joseph Parker that he was a self-made man, Parker commented: "Well, sir, that relieves the Lord of a great responsibility."

V. HAMAN'S CRAFTINESS (5:14)

At the suggestion of his wife and friends Haman ordered a gallows to be built from which to hang Mordecai. Why not get the king's permission to hang Mordecai the first thing in the morning? Then he could really enjoy the banquet with the king. After all, the king had already approved the plan for the early destruction of the whole Jewish nation. Such an insignificant matter as the execution of one Jew would, of course, be sanctioned by the king especially since the request had come from his favorite minister.

It appeared quite likely that Ahasuerus would have granted Haman's request, but for one highly improbable incident that happened that night. The king had insomnia, could not sleep, and remembered the plot to take his life, which had been discovered by a loyal subject. What great consequences turn on seemingly insignificant happenings. "Man proposes, but God disposes." Chapter 6 gives the development.

Chapter 6

HAMAN'S HUMILIATION (6:1-14)

The king, having a sleepless night, asked that the "book of the records of the chronicles" be brought and read to him. Possibly it was thought that the sound of a man's voice reading aloud would bring sleep to the king. Actually the hand of God in providential leading was soon to be evident. "Here is a remarkable instance of the veiled providential control of God over circumstances of human history. Upon the king's insomnia, humanly speaking, were hinged the survival of the chosen nation, the fulfillment of prophecy, the coming of the Redeemer, and therefore the whole work of redemption. Yet the outcome was never in doubt; for God was in control, making the most trivial of events work together for Haman's defeat and Israel's preservation."[1]

I. THE REMEMBRANCE THAT WAS LONG OVERDUE (6:1-4)

The point at which the king's sleepless night occurred is at the very center of the history of the book of Esther. It was also the night between the two banquets which Esther had scheduled. It was almost a foregone conclusion that Haman would receive permission from King Ahasuerus in the morning for Mordecai to be hanged on the prepared gallows. Of course, no one but Haman knew of his plan for the hanging of Mordecai.

Another seeming coincidence in the reading of the chronicles was that the history read contained the account of Bigthan's and Teresh's plot against the king. Mordecai's name consequently came before the king who immediately asked, "What honor and dignity hath been bestowed upon Mordecai for this? Then said the king's servants who ministered unto him, There has nothing been done for him" (6:3).

This was an inexcusable oversight on the part of the king, and was, in fact, a gross neglect of Persian law. Attention must

---

[1] *New Scofield Reference Bible,* p. 566.

immediately be given to correct this oversight and inconsistency. Early morning had apparently by now arrived and the king, anxious to remedy his wrong asked, "Who is in the court?" None other than Haman was there. He had come early to secure the king's permission for Mordecai's hanging.

We may again mark the providential hand of God, the One who "slumbers not nor sleeps." The king's mind was on Mordecai following his sleepless night. Haman's mind was also on Mordecai, but for a completely different reason. The king desired to honor and reward Mordecai, while Haman wanted to see him hanged.

II. THE RECOGNITION THAT WAS WELL DESERVED (6:5-11)

"And the king said, Let him come in" (6:5). "So Haman came in" (6:6). Immediately upon seeing Haman the king asked him, "What shall be done for the man whom the king delighteth to honor" (6:6). Poor Haman was completely taken in by the king's question! Who but himself would the king want to honor? Why he was the king's favorite and was going to share another banquet with the king that very day! His pride and vanity must be satisfied. His delight knew no bounds. The thing that would please him the most would be to be publicly honored by the king so that all in the city could see how well thought of he was. So he suggested that the man whom the king wanted to honor should "wear the king's royal apparel, ride on the king's horse, wear the royal crown, and be led through the city for all to see" (6:8, 9).

To Haman's utter consternation, the king instructed him to do for Mordecai exactly as he had suggested (6:10). Surely there must be some mistake! Haman could not believe what he had heard that Mordecai was the one to be so honored. This was to be done for the man whom Haman had expected to see hanged on the gallows? Here is a perfect example of how the "expectation of the wicked is cut short."

Mordecai allowed himself to be honored by the king as Haman put the proposed plan into operation. For him it was no doubt only an empty ceremony, but he could see it as an evidence of God's hand upon him. It would mark the turning point in his hope to save his people. It would bring encouragement to Queen Esther and strengthen her determination to save her people. It would also have a positive effect upon the king.

III. THE RECOMPENSE THAT WAS COMPLETELY UNEXPECTED (6:12-14)

Following the public parade honoring him, Mordecai returned to the king's gate (6:12). For him, the public acclaim was but a passing incident. For Haman, forced to carry out the public honoring of Mordecai, the whole affair was by now a sickening experience of complete and utter devastation and humiliation. With his head covered, he returned home in mourning to tell his wife Zeresh and his friends what had befallen him (6:13).

He had gone forth early that morning with the confidence that his plan for Mordecai's removal would be approved by the king. He returned defeated and frightened, realizing that not only had his plan been a complete failure but that his own life would now be in jeopardy. His "wise men" said to him that "if Mordecai was of the seed of the Jews, before whom thou hast begun to fall, thou shalt not prevail against him, but shalt surely fall before him" (6:13). What ominous words! They proved to be prophetic of the downfall of Haman and his house. He saw his own gallows before his eyes!

While they were still discussing the fateful turn of events with Haman, the king's chamberlain arrived to bring Haman to the banquet that Esther had prepared (6:14).

"The Lord raiseth those who are bowed down" (Ps. 146:8). History is "His story." God is on the throne and men and movements must do His bidding.

Chapter 7

HAMAN HANGED (7:1-10)

The king, Haman, and Queen Esther were now together at
the second banquet which had been scheduled. Esther had told
the king that at the second banquet she would tell him what her
petition was. At Persian banquets such as this the time was
spent mainly in drinking and eating rich desserts. The solid
dishes were few. The king now asked Esther for the third time
to tell him of her petition.

I. THE PETITION THAT SECURED THE KING'S APPROVAL (7:1-6)

Note first of all that Esther spoke *courteously* to the king.
She knew that the time had now come for her to unburden her
heart. She could no longer delay in presenting her petition to
the king. She had learned not only when to be silent, but when
to speak. "If I have found favor in thy sight, O king, and if it
please the king . . ." (7:3). She recognized her opportunity, but
did not seek to take advantage of it.

In the second place, Esther spoke *clearly*. She made known
to the king exactly her position. "Let my life be given me at
my petition, and my people at my request; For we are sold, I
and my people, to be destroyed, to be slain, and to perish"
(7:3, 4). Esther now revealed her own nationality. She did not
ask selfishly that she and Mordecai alone be spared, but that the
whole nation of the Jews would be delivered from death and
destruction.

We are reminded from the New Testament of the Apostle
Paul's similar concern for his people when he said, "Brethren,
my heart's desire and prayer to God for Israel, is that they might
be saved" (Rom. 10:1). His prayer was that the darkness
might be taken from their eyes and that they might see the salvation of the Lord.

Finally, Esther spoke *convincingly*. The life or death of the
people of God throughout all of the provinces of Persia de-
pended on the outcome of Esther's plea before the king. He
could not fail to sense the deep emotion and concern with which

Esther spoke. She indicated that it was not just as slaves that they were being sold. This of itself would have caused Esther to refrain from her petition (7:4). However, this fact alone would have caused loss to the king, for a free people would be of more value to the king than a nation of slaves (7:14). Her people were to be "destroyed, to be slain, and to perish." This was more than just repetitive language by which Esther hoped to move the king's heart. It expressed the deep involvement of Esther with her people.

II. THE PROTECTION THAT SPARED A NATION'S PEOPLE (7:5-8)

"Then the king, Ahasuerus, said unto Esther the queen, Who is he, and where is he, who would presume in his heart to do so? And Esther said, The adversary and enemy is this wicked Haman" (7:5, 6).

Though the king asked the question, he could not really be in any doubt of whom Esther was speaking. Upon hearing the name Haman, the king "arising from the banquet of wine in his wrath went into the palace garden" (7:7). No doubt he wanted to recover from his initial anger and give himself time for some sober reflection on what course of action to pursue.

At the same time, Haman arose from the table to plead with the queen to spare his life. He knew that he could expect no mercy from the king, but no doubt hoped that he could secure some favor from the more tenderhearted queen. He threw himself upon the couch where Esther was reclining, perhaps even grasping her feet as was common practice on the part of those seeking mercy. At this point the king returned, and observing what he thought was a compromising position on the part of Haman, cried out, "Will he force the queen also before me in the house? As the word went out of the king's mouth, they covered Haman's face" (7:8). This was customarily done to a condemned man indicating that he was no longer even worthy to see the light of day.

III. THE PROCLAMATION THAT SLEW A WICKED PRINCE (7:9, 10)

Harbonah, one of the chamberlains, then informed the king of the gallows that Haman had already prepared for Mordecai. When the king heard this, he said, "Hang him on it" (7:9). He was subsequently hanged, and "the king's wrath was pacified" (7:10).

As one considers the ignominious conclusion to what appeared originally as a brilliant career for the man Haman, it seems that such severe retribution was justified. The most bitter result of the fateful story was that Haman was hanged on his own gallows which he had prepared for the execution of another. We are often troubled and confused when we see the apparent success and prosperity of the wicked. We must always remember that sin will eventually meet its due reward. "Sin when it is finished bringeth forth death." "The mills of God grind slowly, but they grind exceeding small. With patience he stands waiting, but with exactness grinds he all."

A story is told of an irreverent, ungodly farmer who boasted to his friends that he had plowed a field on Sunday, sowed the seed on Sunday, cultivated on Sunday, and finally had harvested the crop and placed it in his barns on an October Sunday. To top his boast he stated that his crop was the biggest and best in the entire community. All of this he claimed showed that reverence for God and trust in His goodness had no basis whatever. A Christian farmer in the community upon hearing the ungodly man's boast quietly replied, "Let our friend remember that God doesn't settle all of his accounts in the month of October."

"He made a pit and digged it, and is fallen into the ditch which he made. His mischief shall return upon his own head, and his violent dealing shall come down upon his own pate" (Ps. 7:15, 16).

Chapter 8

PROGRAM PROSPERED (8:1-17)

Immediately following the execution of Haman action was taken to dispose of his property, and to secure someone to fill his office.

I. THE PROMOTION THAT MORDECAI RECEIVED (8:1, 2)

In the Persian system of law and order when a criminal was executed, his entire property automatically reverted to the government, and could be disposed of as pleased the king. "On that day did the king, Ahasuerus, give the house of Haman, the Jews' enemy, unto Esther, the queen" (8:1). This no doubt meant that Esther was given control of Haman's house with all that pertained to it, including all of the contents, furniture, treasures, holdings, and even servants.

It is of interest to note that Haman is here called "the enemy of the Jews," a designation which occurs again in Chapter 9, verses 10 and 24. His name still evokes recognition as one of the most notorious Anti-Semites of all history.

Mordecai "came before the king," since by now Esther had told the king about him and their relationship as cousins. There was no longer any reason or need to conceal his nationality. The king took off his ring which he had taken from Haman at the time of his execution, and gave it to Mordecai. This symbolic act indicated that now Mordecai was to assume Haman's position as being second to the king in the affairs of the government and in rule.

Esther at the same time "set Mordecai over the house of Haman" (8:2). No doubt it would not have been proper for Esther to give to Mordecai what she had just received from the king, i.e., the house of Haman, but she could turn it over to Mordecai for his occupancy and use.

II. THE PLEA THAT ESTHER BROUGHT TO THE KING (8:3-6)

Once again Queen Esther found it necessary to appear before

the king to appeal for the life and security of her people. The law for which Haman had secured the king's approval, namely, the destruction of the Jews, was still in force. This law had been signed and sealed on the 13th of the month Nisan (3:12) and was to be put into effect on the 13th of the month Adar. Persian law could not be altered nor reversed (8:8) so the Jews were still very much in danger of execution.

Realizing this, Esther appealed to the king (8:3). She used her womanly tears to good effect, the king held out the golden scepter to her, and she besought the king's favor. Esther asked first for the reversal of the law, suggesting that it was the writing only of Haman (8:5). She added that she could not "endure to see the evil that would come to her people," nor to "see the destruction of my kindred" (8:6).

III. THE PROCEDURE THAT THE KING SUGGESTED FOR THE JEWS (8:7-14)

The king responded to Esther's impassioned plea by reminding her that he had had Haman executed and then had given his house to her. But what had been "written in the king's name, and sealed with the king's ring" (8:8), was irreversible. In effect, however, the king indicated that they could have the liberty to devise some type of action to save the Jews, but that he could not retract his decree nor break what was a cardinal principle of Persian law. He apparently did not want to be bothered further, but gave Esther and Mordecai full permission to write a law that would satisfy them and make possible the sparing of the lives of the Jews.

Mordecai lost no time in calling in the king's scribes. On the 23rd day of the month Sivan, he "wrote in the name of King Ahasuerus," sealed the writing with the king's ring and sent out the decree by "posts on horseback, and riders on mules, camels, and young dromedaries" (8:10), to the governors and princes of the 127 provinces of the Persian realm extending from India to Ethiopia.

The decree gave permission "to the Jews who were in every city to gather themselves together, and to defend their lives, to destroy, to slay, and to cause to perish, all of the power of the people and province that would assault them, both little ones and women, and to take the property of them for spoil, Upon one day in all the provinces of King Ahasuerus, namely, upon the thirteenth day of the twelfth month, which is the month Adar" (8:11, 12).

The decree was given at Shushan the palace and sent throughout the entire realm.

IV. THE PROGRAM THAT CHARACTERIZED THE JEWS' CELEBRATION (8:15-17)

Mordecai, following the sending forth of the decree, departed from the palace attired in "royal apparel of blue and white, wearing a crown of gold, and a garment of fine linen and purple" (8:15). The whole city "rejoiced and was glad" when they saw him. "The Jews had light, and gladness, and joy, and honor" (8:16). All Jewry throughout the entire Persian realm could now rejoice over being relieved from the terrible fear that had hung over them.

Everywhere the news was received with joy and gladness. The Jews prepared special feasts and rejoiced in the good news. The day was made a holiday. "And many of the people of the land became Jews; for the fear of the Jews fell upon them" (8:17). The people now realized that the Jews had the law on their side. This caused many to want to become a part of the Jewish people. Perhaps they reasoned that the Jews might take revenge on all who were not on their side. Hence they became "proselytes" to the Jewish faith. Whether or not this was a matter of convenience or whether they really worshipped the true and living God is a matter of conjecture.

VENTURE VICTORIOUS (9:1-32)

As the zero hour approached for the confrontation of the Jews with their enemies, there apparently was extensive preparation made on both sides. "The Jews gathered themselves together in their cities throughout all the provinces" (9:2). Their enemies no doubt did likewise. There were two armed camps as it were, prepared and awaiting the appointed day of conflict.

I. THE ENDORSEMENT OF THE PROCLAMATION (9:1-4)

It appeared that from the very outset the Jews would have the advantage. "The enemies of the Jews hoped to have power over them (though it was turned to the contrary, that the Jews had rule over them that hated them)" (9:1). By this time Mordecai's position was well known throughout the capital and the realm, and his power and authority were well established and respected. The princes, deputies, governors, and officers of the king endorsed the position of the Jews and lent their support to Mordecai. They had decided to give their moral support to the side of the Jews in the forthcoming civil disturbance.

Mordecai had not only governed wisely, but his influence became stronger before the king and consequently he enjoyed a good reputation and standing through the entire realm. It was the part of the stronger party.

II. THE ENFORCEMENT OF THE PROVISIONS (9:5-16)

The legislation that had been drawn up by Mordecai and Queen Esther, approved by the king, and communicated throughout the realm provided for the encounter between the Jews and their enemies to take place on the 13th day of the month Adar.

The Jews apparently took the offensive and attacked the enemy with "sword and slaughter" (9:5). In Shushan the palace they slew 500 men. Included among those killed were the ten sons of Haman. A report of the number killed in Shushan was brought to the king. He then inquired of Esther if she had any further petition to make of him. She requested that a second day of conflict be permitted, and that the ten sons of Haman who had been killed should be hanged on the gallows. The king gave his permission. On the 14th day of Adar, 300 more were slain at Shushan, and the sons of Haman were placed on the gallows.

It may seem that this request of Esther's was revengeful. However, we may not know the whole story. Apparently she was concerned that the Jews might do a complete "house-cleaning" and thus would be more likely to free themselves from any further persecution by their foes. The hanging of the ten sons of Haman indicated that they had died in deep disgrace. It was not uncommon among the Persians to inflict this type of public humiliation upon persons who had been killed in some other way.

Outside of Shushan, the record indicates that some 75,000 were slain in the rest of the Persian Empire (9:16). (Let it be noted that in the Septuagint translation of Esther the number slain outside of Shushan is given as 15,000 rather than 75,000. This figure seems to be more in keeping with the figure of 500 for the number slain at Shushan.)

It is most interesting and significant to note that though the decree permitted the Jews "to take the property of their enemies for spoil" (8:11), this they did not do. We are told three times over in verses 10, 15, and 16 of Chapter 9 that the Jews who were victorious did not even touch ("laid not their hand") the property of their enemies. Apparently, they wanted all to know that they were not out to plunder and rob, but were only concerned about making certain that they would be spared any future persecution.

III. THE ESTABLISHMENT OF THE FEAST OF PURIM (9:17-32)

When the conflict was all over it was natural for the Jews to want to rest and then celebrate their victory. The Jews who lived in the capital had waged the battle on two days, the 13th and 14th of Adar while the Jews in the rest of the provinces had only fought on the one day, the 13th of Adar. Queen Esther and Mordecai, in order to resolve the dilemma of which day should be kept as a memorial of victory, actually proclaimed both days, the 14th and 15th, to be set aside for the proper observance and fitting celebration (9:21, 22). This was to become an annual observance, "that they should keep the fourteenth day of the month Adar, and the fifteenth day of the same, yearly, As the days in which the Jews rested from their enemies, and the month which was turned unto them from sorrow to joy, and from mourning into a good day; that they should make them days of feasting and joy, and of sending portions one to another, and gifts to the poor" (9:21, 22).

The observance became known as the "Feast of Purim" from the word "Pur" which referred to Naman's "casting of lots" (3:7). This became a Jewish national observance and remains today as one of the most hallowed and honored observances. It is observed in the early spring, a month before the Passover, the 14th and 15th of the month Adar. The day preceding these two days of feasting is kept as a day of fasting in observance and commemoration of Queen Esther's going in uninvited before the king to seek his help in saving the lives of her people (4:16).

In order to make certain that the observance would be perpetuated, Queen Esther and Mordecai issued a decree throughout the 127 provinces of the Persian Kingdom for the keeping of the Feast of Purim. "And the decree of Esther confirmed these matters of Purim, and it was written in the book" (9:32). (No doubt this has reference to the book of the chronicles of the realm.)

Other Jewish festivals, observances, and holy days were given to the people by the express proclamation of God through His prophets and leaders. The Feast of Purim was instituted by the authority of Queen Esther and Mordecai, but no doubt under the sanction and approval of God. The Feast of Purim is religiously observed by devout Jews to this day. The observance is ushered in by a period of fasting. This is followed by a synagogue service when the roll or scroll of the Book of Esther is unrolled and solemnly read aloud to all the assembled worshippers. Following the service the Jews return to their homes for a great feast, followed by rejoicing and merry-making and the giving of presents.

Chapter 10

MORDECAI'S MASTERY (10:1-3)

The greatness of King Ahasuerus has been referred to several times throughout the book of Esther. The concluding word about the king has to do with his levying a tribute or tax upon his entire realm, "upon the land and upon the seacoasts" (10:1). Perhaps this indicated some kind of tax reform instituted even under Mordecai's leadership. For further evidence of Ahasuerus' greatness we are referred to "the book of the chronicles of the kings of Media and Persia" (10:2). But it is really the author's intention in these closing verses of the book to place before the reader again the consideration of Mordecai's greatness and influence, his wisdom and philanthropic character.

I. HIS POSITION (10:3)

Mordecai's life displayed true greatness. He had been marked for death, but rose to the highest position in the realm, "next to King Ahasuerus" (10:3). He had evidenced steadfast faith and courage in the days when it appeared that the Jews were marked for extinction. He had been elevated in position so that he could represent his people and help to determine their destiny. His faith had been in God.

II. HIS POPULARITY (10:3)

He was "great among the Jews, and accepted by the multitude of his brethren" (10:3). He did not seek popularity for popularity's sake. He was not one who had set out to deliberately win the admiration and acclaim of the crowds. His being accepted by the "multitude of his brethren," indicated, however, something of his spiritual and moral worth. He had become the champion of his people.

III. HIS PURPOSE (10:3)

He sought "the welfare of his people, and spoke peace to all his seed" (10:3). His purpose was not the elevation of self, but rather the improvement of the status of his persecuted brethren.

Probably the reference to Mordecai's "speaking peace to all his seed," had a primary reference to the gentleness and kindness of his personality and disposition. But the statement may also be enlarged to refer to the maintenance of peace and harmony throughout the realm. To advocate and actively promote peace is to be a benefactor of mankind. Mordecai was evidently this kind of ruler. "Blessed are the peacemakers, for they shall be called the children of God" (Matthew 5:9).

CONCLUSION

Thus has been briefly traced the thrilling history of the people of God. The book of Esther relates how God for His own purposes spared His people through the intervention of Mordecai and Esther. The story has lasting and permanent value especially in the institution of the Feast of Purim which to this day keeps alive in the experience of the Jewish people the recognition of how God delivered them from certain destruction. Had it not been for the establishment of the Feast of Purim, the remembrance of deliverance might well have been forgotten.

As has been noted, though the name of God is not mentioned in the book (possibly because of respect and reverence for the Divine Name), His presence and providence are nowhere more evident than in this history.

May we who live in this day of spiritual and moral declension find the example for courage to believe that we as Esther have "come to the Kingdom for such a time as this," and that if "we perish, we perish," but that we can do no less than be true to our God. Today's world needs men and women who would rather be "right than rich, would rather starve than steal, and who would rather die than lie."

BIBLIOGRAPHY

Holy Bible: *The New Analytical Bible,* John A. Dickson Publishing Co., Chicago, 1941.

Holman Study Bible, Revised Standard, A. J. Holman Co., 1962.

Living Lessons of Life and Love, Paraphrased by Kenneth N. Taylor, Billy Graham Evangelistic Association.

The New Scofield Reference Bible, Oxford University Press, New York, 1967.

Clarke's Commentary, Volume II, Abingdon-Cokesbury Press, New York.

Davis, John D., *A Dictionary of the Bible,* The Westminster Press, 1940. Reprinted Baker Book House.

Dickson, *The New Analytical Bible,* Chicago, 1941.

Hastings, James, *The Great Texts of the Bible,* Deuteronomy to Esther, Charles Scribner's Sons, New York, 1011.

Hayden, Eric W., *Preaching through the Bible,* Vol. 2. Zondervan Publishing House, Grand Rapids, Michigan, 1967.

Henry, Matthew, *Commentary on the Whole Bible,* Volume II, Fleming H. Revell Co., New York.

Knight, Walter B., *Illustrations for Christian Service,* Wm. B. Eerdmans Publishing Co., Grand Rapids, Michigan, 1949.

Leonard, Wyona Farquhar, *Love That Lasts a Lifetime,* Round Table Press, Manhasset, New York.

Macartney's Illustrations, Clarence E. Macartney, Abingdon-Cokesbury Press, New York.

Mauro, Philip, *Ruth: The Satisfied Stranger,* Hamilton Bros., Boston, 1920.

Meyer, F. B., *Our Daily Homily,* Fleming H. Revell Co., Westwood, N. J., 1966.

Meyer, F. B., *Through the Bible Day by Day,* A Devotional Commentary, Volumes II and IV, American Sunday School Union, 1916.

Morgan, G. Campbell, *The Analyzed Bible,* Fleming H. Revell Co., Westwood, N.J., 1964.

Morgan, G. Campbell, *Living Messages of the Books of the Bible,* Fleming H. Revell, New York, 1912.

Petrie, Arthur, *Ruth the Redeemed,* Fourth Edition, Seattle, Washington.

Pulpit Commentary, Volumes 8 and 15, Wilcox and Follett Co., Chicago.

Ryle, J. C., *Expository Thoughts on the Gospels,* Robert Carter and Brothers, New York, 1867.

Simeon, Charles, *Expository Outlines on the Whole Bible,* Volumes 3 and 4, Zondervan Publishing Co., Grand Rapids, Michigan, 1956.

Spurgeon, C. H., *My Sermon Notes,* Outlines of Discourses — Genesis to Proverbs — Funk and Wagnalls, New York, 1891.

The Sermon Bible, Genesis to II Samuel, Funk and Wagnalls Co., New York.

The Sermon Bible, I Kings to Psalm LXXVI, Funk and Wagnalls Co., New York.